M000024906

WRITERS REPUBLIC

20/21

20-YEARS OF WAR FROM MY EYES

VICTORIA GOMEZ

WRITERS REPUBLIC L.L.C.
515 Summit Ave. Unit R1
Union City, NJ 07087, USA

Website: *www.writersrepublic.com*
Hotline: *1-877-656-6838*
Email: *info@writersrepublic.com*

Ordering Information:
Quantity sales. Special discounts are available on quantity purchases by corporations, associations, and others. For details, contact the publisher at the address above.

Library of Congress Control Number:	2022931848	
ISBN-13:	978-1-64620-915-6	[Paperback Edition]
	979-8-88536-166-8	[Hardback Edition]
	978-1-64620-916-3	[Digital Edition]

Rev. date: 02/14/2022

Book Description

"Thank you for your service."

Such a simple phrase to show appreciation to our military soldiers for volunteering to serve their country. But what about the spouse?

The Global War on Terrorism (GWOT) was a war that U.S. service members participated in for twenty years. In those twenty years, families learned to survive multiple deployments, memorial service after memorial service, several moves, mental health stressors, and a pandemic.

What does the military life look like from the lens of military spouses who had to endure all of those challenges and more? What does the military wife sacrifice to support her soldier's career? The military life and deployment are equally hard on the family as they are on the soldier.

This book is an intimate look at the Global War on Terrorism from 2001 to 2021 from the military spouses' perspective; all of the heartache and the joy told through stories, letters, and interviews from military spouses.

Prologue

Inhale . . . exhale . . . and breathe.

Seems like just yesterday and a lifetime ago—twenty years.

I have a wooden wall sign on my desk that says "Live a GREAT story" in big, white letters. There's no greater story to tell than that of being a military wife during the last twenty years of the Global War on Terrorism.

"Thank your husband for his service."

That seems to be the first sentence out of anyone's mouth when I show my military ID card. I stare a little too long at the cashier, and I catch myself.

"I will let him know." And I smile.

She politely continues to scan and bag my items, and I can't help but think that this sweet, young lady, who wasn't even born in 2001, probably has no clue how twenty years ago, my world was turned upside down.

On September 6, 2021, five days before the twentieth anniversary of the September 11 attacks on the World Trade Center Towers, the U.S. Department of Defense published the Immediate Release Casualty Status report.

Here are some hard-to-swallow facts:

Operation Iraqi Freedom U.S. Casualties:

Military – 4,418

KIA – 3,418

Non-hostile – 937

Wounded – 31,994

Operation New Dawn U.S. Casualties:

KIA – 38

Non-hostile – 36

Wounded – 298

Operation Enduring Freedom U.S. Casualties:

Afghanistan

KIA – 1,833

Non-hostile – 385

Wounded – 20,093

Other locations:

KIA – 12

 Non-hostile – 118

WIA – 56

Operation Inherent Resolve (Bahrain, Cyprus, Egypt, Iraq, Israel, Jordan, Kuwait, Lebanon, Qatar, Saudi Arabia, Syria, Turkey, and United Arab Emirates):

KIA – 20

Non-hostile – 86

WIA – 269

Operation Freedom Sentinel (U.S. Casualties in Afghanistan after December 21, 2014):

KIA – 77

Non-hostile – 30

WIA – 597

As I register the total loss and wounded from twenty years of war, I can't help but reflect on my family's involvement. I keep thinking about numbers . . . numbers . . .

I walk to my car, and I pull out my journal, and I keep thinking: twenty years.

Holy shit . . . Has it been twenty years since we started this war?

I still remember the day this nightmare all began. I got called into my boss' office, and my best friend held my hand as we watched live events unfold as the second plane crashed into the second Twin Tower. He clenched my hand harder, nails digging in, and I looked at him, tears streaming down both of our faces.

I could barely breathe. Our entire office had stopped working. Over 200 people stopped moving, and all you could hear was the air conditioning unit in the building running. I was glued to the pixelated images on the TV, and all I could think was, "We are going to war."

I was an Army officer at the time, and I was twenty-four years old.

Frozen in that moment in time, I'm now hysterically sobbing in the Old Navy parking lot.

As I attempt to collect my thoughts, here are the numbers that pop into my head from 2001 to 2021:

6 deployments

10 moves

3 missed weddings

7 missed anniversaries

5 missed Christmases

15 total missed birthdays

1 missed first step

6 missed Super Bowls

Countless missed kids' games, plays, awards, school dances, discussions about girls, questions about life and death.

Lots of missed time together.

These numbers all came at the price of my soldier's time deployed. Unfortunately, this does not include the "other" times missed while my soldier was away in the field, training in preparation for deployment.

As I finally started my drive home, I passed by our sons' high school and saw that yellow ribbons were tied around the trees. The yellow ribbons were a part of a local fundraiser, but in my head, the yellow ribbons reminded me of the military wives who tied yellow ribbons around trees to remember their men who were serving overseas. Again, this triggered a sense of sadness, loss, and longing.

I noticed that the flags were at half-mast.

Just two days before, thirteen marine soldiers were killed by a suicide bomber on Thursday, August 27, 2021. This tragically happened days after the U.S. started pulling all Americans out of Afghanistan. And, once again, the familiar feeling of fear, uncertainty, dread, and sadness overwhelmed me.

My soldier will retire from twenty-two years of serving in the Army. There will be no more moves, no more deployments, and no more missed celebrations. There are no more deliberate day-drinking parties to cope with all of the sadness; no more Friday hodge-podge happy hours where dinner is a collection of frozen food items and lots of wine; and there are no more hails and farewells, dinner parties, balls, memorial services and soldier funerals.

We have chosen a quiet town in the middle of our country to call home.

One of our gracious neighbors looked at me with empathetic eyes when she found out I was a military wife.

She said, "I don't know how you did it. I couldn't have done that moving all of the time and raising the kids by myself."

I didn't think about what she said until that evening. It resonated with me: I couldn't have done it either without the military spouses along this journey who became my adopted sisters . . . my family.

Over the last twenty years, there's very little written about the Global War on Terrorism (GWOT) wives, husbands, partners who are at home handling the house, dealing with the kids, balancing work, and balancing unit responsibilities. There's little-to-nothing published about the wives' sleepless nights, anxiety, alcohol consumption, hospital visits, and multiple memorial services and funerals attended. No one ever asks the wife about how she feels about the war or how she's doing after twenty years of multiple moves and deployments. Is it possible for a wife to have post-traumatic stress disorder after 20-years of being married to a soldier?

If life is described as a journey with blips and bumps on the road, then I would describe the military wife's life as an adventure taken in a Southeast Asian bus stuffed with people speaking different languages. She can't see where she's going, and the truck is driven on uneven roads with crater-sized potholes. But she's stuffed in the bus, riding along, holding on for dear life wondering which stop she's supposed to get off at

I started to obsess about this life I've lived. I called a friend and asked her how she felt about me collecting stories and telling the military wife's version of the last twenty years.

Enthusiastically, she said, "Wouldn't that be something? Wouldn't that be something to tell our side of the story? You should do it."

With that, I was inspired.

If our soldier's service and sacrifice is 75% of the story, then the GWOT spouses at home have the other 25%. This book is a collection of the 25% to give clarity to the entire spectrum.

This is an ode to the GWOT military spouses and partners who voluntarily shared the good, the bad, and ugly. I don't think the movies or the reality shows do a very good job of portraying the military wives' selfless service and their personal battles on the home front.

This is a collection of anecdotal stories of military wives that have battled through and survived the military life. It is my hope that I am able to tell their stories. I hope to give a greater understanding of what challenges wives and families have faced and all that they have sacrificed along the way.

I want to thank you, sisters and brothers, for your service.

***Disclaimer: The term "military wives" refers to wives, husbands, and same-gender couples that have married into the military. I honor all spouses who have supported and served alongside their service members. Whether it's one year or thirty years, I honor you all.

To the military spouses who have held my hand and battled with me on this journey through hell and back while our soldiers defended our country: Happy hour is at my house!

2001–2004

S and J

Marrying our soldiers before the deployment was a huge component of practical and functional. My boyfriend did his first deployment to Afghanistan in 2002. I was still a student in college, and it was the most difficult time because communication was very limited then. The unit couldn't tell me what was happening because I was only a girlfriend. I only knew what was happening from the news and his mother.

I started dating J in October 2000. I was still in college. Little did we know that September 11, 2001, would be the catalyst for the decisions we made for the next 10-years. This was only one year after we started dating.

He graduated from Ranger School on September 13, 2001, just two days after 9/11. Being raised a military brat, I knew J was going to have to be deployed. Our country was going to war.

He was deployed shortly after July 4, 2002. I was just a girlfriend, so the unit didn't give me information. Pretty much, all of the information I got were from his letters or the news or the other girlfriends I was friends with.

College kept me busy and distracted. I wrote letters and sent packages. Time passed very slowly.

The unit was redeployed in the Spring of 2003, and shortly after, we were engaged. The exact date: July 30, 2003. We talked about a civil marriage. We talked about the lack of benefits I would receive if something were to happen to him, and so, we decided to get married.

Prior to his second deployment, less than six months after he had gotten home, we got married. We were married on August 7, 2003. The unit chaplain gave our vows. In attendance were a couple of the other lieutenants and their girlfriends.

Our small ceremony with our friends helped prepare us emotionally and logistically for the next deployment. But this time, I was a wife.

I was still at school, but now, I was given updates about his platoon. This was a newly added element of stress to my life . . . I now was given information from the unit about what was happening. I now knew everything that was happening and I didn't know if I wanted to.

D and A

We got married in August 2000. I was twenty years old and my soldier was moving me from Florida to Alaska. I was a new Army wife, away from home for the first time, and in a state that was basically like a new country.

Our son was born on September 5, 2001. We were preparing our family to move to North Carolina. I was so happy because I was getting closer to home and I would be able to see my family often.

On September 9, 2001, A started his trip to New Mexico via ferry and Washington State. We were planning on seeing family in New Mexico before heading east. I was in recovery and preparing to fly to New Mexico.

And then September 11th happened.

I was a new military wife. I was moving for the second time in one year. I had a brand-new baby. And now, our country was at war.

We arrived in North Carolina in November of 2001, and the post had barbed wire all around it. There was heightened security to get on post. And as a new wife, I had no clue what was about to happen or what A was going to have to do. Months leading up to the deployment, A was very busy. His time at home was precious . . .

Our son was only eight months old when A deployed. Again, I was still new to the military, a new mother, and my soldier left me to go to war.

I wrote letters; I wrote lots of letters because they were in such a remote location, and all of the communication systems weren't functioning yet. My letters took forever to get to him. I think my first letters took about six weeks. And that was the same for his letters getting home to me.

All I can say is that our first year of marriage, while I know there are pockets of happiness in there, was tough. If you had asked me what my life was going to be like as an Army wife, I would never have pictured it to be like this.

Marriage is a triumph of imagination over intelligence.
—*Oscar Wilde*

Chapter 1

War Bride

*War bride —a woman who marries a man that she met
while he is on active service during a time of war.*

But couldn't that be a term used for any new bride? Because, when it comes down to it…marriage is a constant battle. Sometimes lines are drawn and there's a winner or a loser. There's surrender and compromise. Coalitions are formed or enemies are created. Skillful tacticians have to be able to anticipate four-to-five maneuvers ahead in order to be prepared for multiple outcomes. Marriage is a delicate battle.

During WWII, over 60,000 foreign, young women reportedly married American soldiers. They got married and hoped to leave their hometowns that were devastated by war to move to America.

Would a young girl marry a soldier if she was told the following: You are marrying an American hero, BUT there is a lot of personal sacrifice that comes with it. First, get used to being alone. Soldiers are always training for war. Inevitably, they will deploy to war and you will be left by yourself. Your entire military-married life will be spent alone and in constant worry. Second, you will have to move A LOT. You will have to move your family every two-to-three years. There will be times where you will have to move your entire house alone because your soldier has to be at his new job early. You will have to learn how to do that. Third, you will be responsible for all of the household duties…that includes enrolling and disenrolling children from schools and sports and hospitals and dentists and specialty clinics.

You will have to ensure that everyone has passports and that the all shot records are current. Lastly, you will have a very difficult time finding a job. Since you are moving so often, finding a job can be a challenge. You will have to figure out how to occupy your time while your soldier is gone.

Would that same young lady have married her soldier if she was told all of this up front?

Like generations past, young, girls married soldiers days before deployment. Immediately following the attacks on the Twin Towers on September 11, 2001, girls became war brides. In the heat of the moment, they married soldiers. They were drunk with the romantic notion of marrying an American hero.

As sick and twisted as this may sound, it was the most romantic act of chivalry. Soldiers married their brides because they wanted to ensure that if something were to happen, they left their wife with their military survivor benefits and incentives (healthcare and insurance).

The bottom line was this: soldiers DIDN'T know if they were coming home, and they wanted to give whatever military financial support they could to their new brides.

July 28, 2003: 3 Doors Down released their power ballad "Here Without You." For the unlucky few, our soldiers were already on their second deployment to Iraq or Afghanistan. At that point in time, the war in the Middle East was only two years old. America was still fueled with patriotism, and our soldiers were voluntarily joining by the hundreds to support the war effort. American citizens were still supporting our soldiers, and banners and welcome signs were hung up all over the airports.

Americans were proud of our soldiers, and we were united by the effort to end terrorism.

Terms like Operation Enduring Freedom and Operation Iraq Freedom were household terms. These terms designated the deployment missions. You couldn't turn the television on without hearing about updates in the Middle East. Citizens were watching the news morning, noon, and night.

Young women were honored to marry an American hero. Young patriots, ignorant of the responsibilities that came with marrying a soldier. Her idealistic definition of a marriage was not what she ended up with.

And there was no one who could outline the sacrifices and concessions she was going to have to make.

Being married for the first time is scary. Being married for the first time and figuring out marital rhythm is challenging. For most marriages, the challenges lie in learning individual intricacies: does he leave the toilet seat up? Does she put the toothpaste cap back on the tube? Why does he leave the dinner dishes in the sink before he goes to bed? Why does she take 45-minutes before bed to moisturize?

Being married for the first time and moving in together can be exciting.

Being married for the first time to a soldier adds an entirely different element of excitement to the relationship. First, moving in together will most likely be followed by moving to a new state or country. Secondly, a soldier's daily routine typically starts at 5:30 a.m. and can end as late as 7:00 pm. There may be pockets of lunch or breakfast dates built in, but typically, meals are earlier or later in the day if the couple wants to dine together. Thirdly, the military spouse doesn't have any friends, can't find employment, and her soldier may deploy. So, she begins her marriage not knowing…not knowing her soldier's schedule, not knowing what her future holds, and not knowing anyone around her.

There is something romantic and fairytale esque about marrying a soldier. Maybe it's just the uniform. But that idealism about marriage disappears very quickly in the military. Unfortunately, this lesson is only learned with time and lots of frustration.

There are many surprises that come unexpectedly to the new military wife. The military bride first learns that she is required to surrender all of her personal contact information to everyone. If she cherishes her privacy, being under the microscope all of the time comes as a cultural shock.

One of the many reasons that the military wife is expected to share her personal contact information (telephone number, address, email) to the unit is simple: this information is used for the unit to give official updates about the soldiers. But the reality sets in—the wife's contact information is so the military knows where and how to contact her in the event that an accident or tragedy were to occur. Basically, the military needed to

3

know how to find the wife if her soldier was wounded or killed. This was especially important in a time of war.

The very reality of his profession sets in: she married a man who could die tomorrow.

And then the questions start to flood in: What does he actually do? What is his JOB? What happens if he does die? What do I do? What is a unit? Why do they need my information? Now what? And why am I stationed in Alaska?

Unfortunately, for the young bride, the first year of marriage to a soldier is overwhelming. In the early stages of GWOT, there were little to no systems in place to help the military spouse adapt to the rapid deployment sequence. Soldiers got married quickly, and immediately following, they deployed leaving their brides home alone. They had to figure out how to be a wife to a soldier...alone.

Liberty Girl is a Norman Rockwell painting from 1943. It's a painting of Rosie, a patriotic woman carrying all of her tools. Rockwell's intent was to convey the importance that women at home played during war. This is absolutely true of the contributions that military wives/spouses have made throughout history. She has battled the balance of life at home so the soldier could fight the war overseas.

The military wife carries all of the home responsibilities while the soldier is in the service. And so, the military wife is critical to the war mission because she is essential in maintaining home-life operations.

What does the military spouse do if something happens to the car and the soldier is in the field? What does a military spouse do if she's working, the soldier is in the field for 3-weeks, she has two-sick children, one has to go to the hospital and stay in the hospital overnight, and the soldier can't come home? Who does she call for help if her soldier can't come home from the field? Overall, there is the unspoken expectation that the military wife is responsible for everything that is associated with the home.

The question is: did she sign up for this?

The young, military wife didn't know that marriage in the military is like being married part-time. The corporation of the Army expects the military spouse to operate at home independently. But no-one tells her that. The corporation of the Army expects the military wife to stay connected with the unit because the military profession, with training and deployments, is very dangerous. It is very important for the military spouse to know who the soldier works with or how to get in touch with the soldier if something tragic happened at home and vice versa.

From the first day of marriage, the young bride enters a high-speed marathon in the middle of the race, and never gets off the race route until the soldier decides it's time to get off. The sad truth for the early GWOT war brides was this: everything she learned only came with time, experience, and if she was lucky, mentorship.

The hardest thing about being a senior ranking soldier's wife during a deployment is the pressure to stay calm and collected when all of the younger wives are crying.

I felt the same way as them. I wanted to scream and yell and curse.

But I couldn't. It was my responsibility to be the pillar of strength. So, I walked around the bus pick-up area and hugged each girl. I held their hands and told them that we had each other and that we now had to be strong. I stood there in silence, listening to the cries and wails, and we watched our soldiers drive away to the airfield.

As I watched the girls walk to their cars and drive away, I felt my heavy heart in my chest. I felt like I floated to my car because I was numb. I drove to Starbucks, and cried in the parking lot for about fifteen minutes by myself.

-Military Wife

. . . May the Lord keep watch between you and me when we are away from each other.

—*Genesis 31:49*

Chapter 2

The First Farewell

It is truly something to have someone so special to say goodbye to.

From 2001 to 2002, the rapid deployment sequence was new to soldiers and families. Soldiers used to get a phone call at all hours of the day and night followed by immediate orders to head to the unit and go into the field for training. Following 9/11, soldiers were getting calls to prepare themselves for deployment. In the early years of the war, soldiers were only given weeks to prepare for deployment.

Soldiers were given short-notice orders (anywhere from three days to less than a month) to deploy. Military wives, girlfriends, fiancées, and family were not ready to send their soldiers off to war, but deployment was real and here.

There was no way to predict when they were going to deploy, but our country had officially declared war, and deployment was inevitable.

Having to say goodbye is never easy. Farewelling a soldier before a deployment is the most gut-wrenching, heart-stabbing experience . . . EVER. This was especially true in the early days of the war.

In the movie "We Were Soldiers," LTC Hal Moore wakes before sunrise and kisses his wife on the head. She pretends to be asleep, and she listens as he walks out of the house onto the street. He pauses on his front stoop, takes a deep breath, and without hesitation, proceeds to walk down the street to the barracks. Buses are staged to pick the soldiers up to take them to the flight line for departure.

With regret, Julia Moore leaps out of bed and runs down the stairs in her nightgown and bare feet out into the street. Tears streaming down her face, she whispers, "I love you," knowing at that moment the very reality all military wives know—that it might be the last time I see him. That scene was Fort Benning, Georgia, 1965.

Fast forward to Fort Bragg, North Carolina, Spring 2002.

Picture this:

An empty field spray-painted and marked with picket signs. Over 1,000 soldiers are filling the area, lining up by company, being inspected by sergeants and senior leaders. This once-empty field where soldiers trained and played football on the weekends is now designated the soldier-ready area. There were soldiers everywhere: sprawled out on their gear, anxiously waiting for the buses to pick them up. Most were fueled on adrenaline, excited, ready to deploy, and most of all to kick the Taliban's ass.

Some were sitting on the ground, lying on their rucksacks quietly. What were they thinking about?

Everything seemed to move in slow motion and quickly all at the same time.

There were some soldiers with their loved ones. There were lots of tears, nervous laughs, hands being held tightly. Kids running up and down the aisles, tripping on bags and equipment.

Soldiers were walking in and out of the company headquarters to sign out their weapons.

There were many moving pieces: duffle bags being loaded onto humongous pallets, sergeants yelling for soldiers to do their equipment checks, soldiers running in and out of the shoppette getting their tobacco products and Slim Jim's. Nervous laughs and profanity. That's all you heard the entire time.

And then there were the women . . .

All around, women were crying hysterically, burying their heads in their soldier's chest. Seasoned wives tried their hardest to stay strong for their kids and soldiers, their faces instantly aging with worry lines. Tears welling up, but they were determined not to show hysteria. Kids young and old were sad and silent, waiting . . . just waiting.

The buses pulled up and the sobs got louder. The bus engines turned off, and immediately, the leaders went into accountability mode.

All of the families hugged and cried and held their soldiers just a little bit longer. There were enough tears shed to fill an Olympic-sized pool. The military police escorts started to direct wives and family to stand back behind the roped off area as soldiers lined up. All you could hear was wailing and sniffling, and names being called out followed by "I love you. Please be careful."

Roll call was called: "Anders! Anders!"

Soldier answered with a loud and thunderous: "Here, First Sergeant!"

"Get on the fucking bus. Load it back to front. Let's go! Baker?!"

"Here, Sergeant." Soldiers started to line up.

"Bean?! . . . Bean?!"

"Here, Sergeant," the soldier yelled with a little crackle in his voice. He kissed his wife one last time and didn't turn around as he moved to the bus line.

"Bellow?!"

"Here, Sergeant."

"All right, airborne! Let's go! Let's go!"

As each soldier loaded the bus, some refused to look out the window at their loved ones, in hopes to disguise their sadness. Others . . . well, other soldiers waved at their loved ones as the bus pulled away.

In the early years of the war, this melancholy farewell scene played on repeat monthly in multiple places all over the world. Military wife sororities initiated members by the hundreds. Complete strangers became sisters instantaneously.

Unlike the movies, though, soldiers didn't just leave on the bus, arrive at the flight line, and get on the planes.

Here's what really happened . . .

The bus arrived at the flight line and soldiers waited around to load the planes. For several hours after they arrived, soldiers waited. They ate snacks, they joked, and took naps. They waited.

The military wife pulled away from the staging area in her car and went home (or to a friend's house) and cried. She cried more. She cried until she couldn't cry anymore. And when she didn't think that it could get any worse, she cried because she couldn't cry. And then she got a call . . .

Her soldier just informed her that there was something wrong with the plane, so their departure was delayed. They were being bussed back to the staging area where family members would have to come back and get them. Their flight now was pushed 24–48 hours.

While the military wife was happy to get an additional day with her soldier, she dreaded having to relive that painful farewell.

She thought, "We already ate at his favorite restaurant. We cried together, and I cried alone. I wore my farewell outfit....shit! What am I going to wear next time? I'm going to have to do this farewell all over again."

For the military wife with young children, this just led to confusion.

"Why is daddy home? Does he still have to still fight the bad guys or does he get to stay home?"

In the early days, the farewells were emotionally and mentally draining. These women, from different backgrounds, different states, different countries, were bonded and baptized with the holy water of painful tears. They had no clue what they had signed up for. From 2002 to 2005, this was the young, military wife's initiation into the *unpredictable hurry-up-and-wait* culture. It was an immediate react-to-contact kind-of-life. And she was just getting a taste of it.

What does that mean?

Without being taught how to do it, she had to be prepared to handle all of the unpredictable changes that the military was going to throw at her. She had to be prepared to change her plans as quickly as she can snap her fingers. She had to be willing to compromise all she wanted and her goals to support her soldier. She had to be ready to pick-up and go or be ready to stay a little bit longer than she wanted.

The first deployment farewell is the most memorable. With all of the emotional pain of saying good-bye, there is the added realty that hits the wife for the first time: this may be her last farewell.

J and J: Our Story; Our First Deployment

We met on November 14, 2000, at the Catholic church we attended when we were both students at Texas A&M University. I was nineteen and he was just shy of twenty-one.

We knew within a month of meeting each other that we would get married. Several months later, after spending the entire summer apart, thanks to his cadet training, we decided it was time to take the next step.

On September 9, 2001, we drove to my hometown to surprise my dad for his birthday. While there, J asked for his permission to marry me. (Thankfully, my dad said yes!) Two days later, 9/11 happened. Six days after that, on September 17, 2001, J asked me to marry him. At the time, I had no idea the extent to which the events of 9/11 would impact the next twenty years of my life.

Prior to his first deployment, my mother-in-law gave each of us journals, so we could document our thoughts and feelings during our time apart. If I'm being honest, reading through my journal was hard. I don't have many good memories from that time in my life, so it was difficult to revisit how scared and lonely I was. Sometimes I wonder how I even got through it.

When J was stationed at a Fort Hood–based unit deployed in January 2004, I was twenty-two years old, living in a one-bedroom apartment in Killeen, had just started a new teaching job, and was twelve weeks pregnant with our first child. I also didn't have a single friend.

Every day was like Groundhog Day: I'd wake up, go to work, come home, eat dinner alone, go to bed, get up the next morning, and do it all over again. It was the loneliest period in my life.

I had forgotten how much he tried to protect me, even while deployed. Reading through my journal entries I noted several times where other spouses would talk about how much danger our husbands were in, but in the rare instances when he could get to a phone, he would always reassure me that things were fine. They were not fine.

We could only speak on the phone once every seven to ten days. Sometimes we spoke more frequently, but other times we'd go two weeks without talking. That was really, really hard.

During J's fourteen-month deployment in OIF II, he was in a HMMWV destroyed by IEDs.

A portion of his journal entry from February 5, 2004, states:

I know my wife and child will be fine. Even if something happens to me, they will be well taken care of.

Here is a portion of one of my journal entries from February 14, 2004, four-and-a-half weeks after Justin was deployed:

I heard on the news that there were riots and protests outside the prison in Abu Ghraib. One protestor held a sign that said, 'Today demonstrations, tomorrow explosions.' Needless to say I have been very worried. My pregnancy hormones were kicking in and I kept crying all day because I miss J and I am so incredibly worried about him.

One morning I woke up and turned on the news only to see that the violence and attacks in my husband's area of operation (AO) were becoming increasingly dangerous.

Here is my journal entry from April 9, 2004:

Today was one of the scariest days of this deployment. I woke up to the news that another convoy was attacked in Abu Ghraib and 9 people were killed. Apparently 2 Soldiers were killed and a couple are unaccounted for. There were also reports that people have been taken hostage there as well. I sat in the apartment in sheer terror waiting for bad news to come, either on the phone or at the door. I am so scared right now and I don't know if I will get to talk to Justin anytime soon.

**Personal reflection of that entry: I remember being so paralyzed with fear that I couldn't even get off the couch. I was just sitting and listening, praying I didn't hear the sound of footsteps coming up to knock on the door of second-floor apartment. I later learned that the attack I referenced occurred when insurgents used RPGs and small-arms fire to attack a U.S. convoy. Apparently J's unit responded to the attack and spent several days engaged in heavy combat. One of the soldiers missing from the attack was SSG M. Maze. His official status was listed as missing-captured and it was nearly four years before his remains were recovered.

A portion of my journal entry from May 2, 2004:

It's hard knowing that the violence in Iraq is as dangerous as ever. 11 Soldiers were killed today. It's times like these that I want J home with me and A. As quickly as time goes by, all of this violence makes the rest of the deployment seem so long.

**I was six months pregnant with A when I wrote the above entry.

A portion of my journal entry from May 27, 2004:

It was very hard attending labor and delivery classes tonight without J. It was a very involved class for the coaches and it made me sad that J wasn't there.

A was born during J's two weeks of R&R during the summer of 2004. The journal entries I included are a bit lengthy, but they are the raw emotions of a newly postpartum twenty-three-year-old who just sent her husband back to war for six-and-a-half more months.

A portion of my journal entry from August 15, 2004:

J left to go back to Iraq this morning. The pain and sadness I felt (and still feel) at having him leave again is indescribable. Our time together was so special and perfect that I almost forgot he was ever gone in the first place and that he had to go back. I am so glad that he was able to be here for A's birth because he was my rock throughout the whole ordeal. I couldn't have made it through without him. The thought of him going back to Iraq for a few more months both scares and saddens me. Saying goodbye to him this time was much harder than last time. I get upset thinking about the things he did with A that he can't do again for a long time. These last 2 weeks have made my love for J grow even stronger. I am immensely happy and blessed to be married to him and could not imagine a better father for my children. He is truly the love of my life.

Journal entry from August 16, 2004:

Today and yesterday have been very hard for me. I break down and cry all the time because I'm absolutely terrified that something bad is going to happen to J. I haven't been able to eat, and the fact that I hardly sleep doesn't help. I am so worried I feel like I can't function sometimes. The 2 weeks we spent together were so perfect, and the thought of losing him makes me sick. I can't live without him. I am so scared right now, but all I can do is pray that he'll be okay.

Finally, my last journal entry on the day of his homecoming, February 25, 2005:

Today's the day! The day we've been waiting for for the last fourteen months! J comes home today! Woohoo! I can't believe we're finally here! I have been imagining this day for so long. This has been a very long and hard journey, but through God's graces we were able to get through it. Only time will tell the true impact our Soldiers made on that country. Hopefully future deployments won't be this lengthy or scary. I have so many emotions going through my body that I can't differentiate between them all. I look forward to what the future holds for J and I and I am anxious to begin the next chapter of our lives.

J went on to deploy three more times, the next one being fifteen months long.

*There are a couple of songs that came out just before he left for those fifteen months that I still cannot listen to because they will instantly make me start crying: "If You're Reading This" by Tim McGraw and "Just a Dream" by Carrie Underwood.

*Once during that deployment, a neighbor knocked on my door at 8:45 at night to bring me something. I was so scared it was a casualty assistance officer that my arms and legs started shaking so bad I could barely make it to the door.

*The night I was informed that two of J's soldiers were killed in an insurgent attack, my four-year-old fell asleep on the couch holding her bedtime books she was waiting for me to read to her but was unable to do so, as I was a mess trying to work out what had happened downrange.

*I didn't realize how stressed I was during that deployment until J came home. Once I knew he was safe and I could finally relax, my entire body went haywire. In the first three months after he returned, I got a stomach bug, strep throat twice, a kidney infection, had two allergic reactions, and ended up in the ER twice.

If there is one thing I have learned in my nineteen-plus years as an Army spouse, it's how important a good support system is. Most of us are not fortunate enough to live near family, so the friends we make along the way become our family. I feel so blessed to have such an amazing Army "family."

Victoria Gomez

Chapter 3

The Day After

The day after the farewell can go one of many ways:

A military spouse wakes up in her same clothes on the couch with one (two or three) empty bottles of wine on the coffee table.

A military spouse may be in her pajamas in her bed, unwilling to get up, eyes swollen from crying, clutching onto her pillow.

A military spouse may wake up at her best friend's house in the clothes she wore the day before, hungover from crying and drinking.

A military spouse awakens in her house, in the same clothes, drives to Burger King for a breakfast sandwich and a Starbucks coffee, and goes home to watch Netflix all day.

A military spouse wakes up, weighs herself, swears that she's going to work-out and lose weight before her soldier redeploys...BUT will not start today!

A military spouse wakes up in her bed, looks over at the empty side of the bed, walks slowly to the bathroom, looks at herself in the mirror, reassures herself that she has to be strong, showers, cries in the shower, changes, and tackles the day.

Regardless of what scenario plays out, there's one truth: the day after the farewell is one of the hardest days for the military family. It is exceptionally hard for the wife.

Some military wives are lucky enough to travel home to their families during the deployment. While it's nice to have that support system at home, sometimes, friends and family can't really comprehend the depth of worry or sadness a wife feels when her soldier is deployed. While moving home to a parent's house while a soldier is deployed can be a great source of comfort, it can also pose many complications.

For example, what does a mother do if her daughter, whose husband is deployed, just starts crying in the middle of a grocery store? Or what does a father do if his grandchildren start crying in the middle of dinner saying that their daddy might die? What does a friend do when her friend refuses to go out and just wants to sit at home and cry all day? What does a young wife do when her parents and friends are constantly harassing her with questions like, "have you heard from him? What's he doing? Are you ok today?"

If the spouse does move home, she has to be able to handle the pressure that comes with it.

There are military spouses that don't move back to their hometown because of the support that they receive from the military community. Moving into a new place and finding friends is very hard. But living in a military installation or a community means that there are almost instant friends right next door. This is not always the case, but at least military families understand the emotional stress and pain of a deployment and are willing to help if a family needs it.

In the early days of the war, communication was sparse. Every day was lived in constant worry or fear. Families didn't know what was happening unless it was on the news.

Spouses waited to get a call or an email from the unit. A favorite song triggered tears. His favorite restaurant made her ache. Everything was a constant reminder that her soldier was gone.

Spouses often got second- or third-hand information about missions from other wives or girlfriends. So, while the military wife learned to live life by herself, her information network became her military sisters. And so, the bond between military spouses, just like their soldiers, became a bond of life or death. The day after a farewell became her battle, and she needed her new military sisters to help her fight. For the military wife with no kids, the challenge becomes how to fill the day with distractions.

If she works, that time temporarily distracts her from being sad. The time she isn't working is when she is lonely. And those times of loneliness can trigger depression. It can also challenge the military wife to find comfort and compassion from others.

As for the military spouse with children, the day after the farewell is a tough fucking day. She is now a mother and a father. How does she handle both roles and all tasks? She immediately becomes the disciplinarian and soother, the judge and jury.

She lived every day in constant fear. Can I do this? Can I take care of myself and my children if my soldier died? How am I going to do this?

Just like her soldier, she was fighting her war every day. She learned very quickly how to multitask. Sit-down dinners were reserved for formal occasions. She learned how to make a variety of crockpot meals to do dinner on the go. She would make dinner, put it in a Tupperware, take the kids to after-school events, and write letters while waiting in the parking lot. She managed the house in survival mode.

Who cuts the grass? Who washes the car? How do you fix a laundry washer and dryer? What bills need to be paid? What school activity is the child in? What fun activities do I need to pencil in on my calendar in between the meetings I should attend for my husband's unit? What deadlines do I have to meet for my job? Can I find a job since this is my third move in five years?

Her days are filled with distractions: kids going to school, unit meetings, after-school activities, and work. Somehow the unwelcomed, single-parenting lifestyle fills the day so she isn't inundated by the stress of her soldier's safety.

It is the same routine every day. And days blend into months.

While the military spouse learns to manage a house by herself, she finds that sprinkled into her day-to-day responsibilities are unit events she is expected to participate in.

These events can include but are not limited to: unit Thanksgiving potluck dinner; kids' Christmas party, volunteer recognition lunches, local community information sessions, etc. etc. The time and space continuum blend days and months like a kaleidoscope. The unit events somehow make the wife and her children feel connected to the other families in the unit that are going through the same challenges. And somehow, all of the lonely, sad families are together and aren't so lonely at that moment.

It's only when the moving stops that the still and quiet become unbearable. She can hear the beating in her eardrums.

Nighttime becomes the military wife's shroud. At night, the world around her collapses, and in her empty, quiet bed, her mind wanders restlessly to thoughts about her soldier. What is he doing? Where is he? Is he safe? Is he eating?

At night, the military wife listens to street sounds, hoping and praying not to hear any car pulling out in front. She has a hard time sleeping for the first week, physically exhausting herself as she juggles all of her newly inherited responsibilities.

And as God is her witness, there is always SOMETHING that goes wrong when the soldier is deployed:

–The check-engine light comes on in the car.

–The laundry dryer dies.

–The child is acting out.

–The dog dies.

–A family member is sick.

She has to figure out how to deal with all of that.

For those that are curious, a typical military family schedule could look like this:

0500:   Wife wakes up to have coffee and enjoy the quiet.

   Walk the dog.

   Run to Wal-Mart if it's in close proximity and buy cookies because she forgot about the class party OR put together a hodgepodge of snacks and call it trail-mix.

0600:   Wake kids

Fight with kids to wake up

Get them changed if needed.

Make breakfast.

0700:   Walk kids to bus stop or load kids up in car for carpool.

If she's a working wife:

0750: Arrive at work and start the day

1347: Get a call from school that child is sick; leave work early to pick up child and take them home.

1513: Check-engine light comes on in the car.

1530: Other children come home; try to get them ready for sports and after-school activities.

1730: Start carpool rodeo with other military families.

1800: Volunteer to attend unit meeting to assist military spouses and figure unit community events.

1817: Start thinking about dinner! CRAP! Start thinking about dinner.

1900: Get kids from all activities.

1930: Do take-out dinner because she forgot about dinner.

2030: Check to ensure all homework is done and send everyone to bed.

2100: Pour a large glass of wine and sit in front of the computer to send an email to military families in the unit or military wives about coffee at Starbucks; shop online.

2213: Head to the bedroom or lie on the couch.

2300: Try to fall asleep.

0131: Try to fall asleep.

There are modifications to every military family schedule, but a regimented schedule keeps everyone organized. The super motivated military spouse will somehow fit a workout in to this busy schedule, too.

Regardless, somehow the military wife balances everything gracefully. Running on fumes, she successfully manages all responsibilities.

And while every military wife's "day after" may look different, there is one constant, and that is the end of week, rotating ad hoc happy hour at the neighbor's house! In true village mentality, the end of week potluck-style happy hour dinners started because military families realized that having dinner together with other kids running around was a great way for wives to decompress and talk to one another about their past week's challenges. These became informal therapy sessions for all members of the family. And after a week of cooking and cleaning, and driving, and watching games, and working, ordering a pizza, drinking a glass of wine, and just laughing with friends was a great temporary hiatus from being sad.

This is how the military wife survived the day-after. She learned very quickly that she couldn't operate independently for an extended period of time, and she was going to have to let her guard down and ask for help if she needed it. She needed her sisters and neighbors for her weekly therapeutic, end-of-week survivor counsel.

It is the day after the deployment that sets the tone for the rest of the deployment. The GWOT military wife at the beginning stages of the war who felt that the day-after was the worst day of her life could never have predicted that her life was going to include many more *days-after* to come.

S and J, University of Virginia, 2002

Hello, WIFE.

How's everything going? I hope school is well and you're wrapping things up, so we can be a family together again.

I got your first letter today! It was dated the 12th of August! That's a two-week delivery time-about; that's about the same for Afghanistan. I was so happy when I got it because it was totally unexpected.

Things here are going alright. It's still unbearably hot out. Hopefully, the winter will come and cool things off soon. SSG C got in today. It's good to have him here because it sucks being alone sometimes. For this first mission, I'll be staying at the airport (BIAP-Baghdad International Airport). This mission could be as long as 3-weeks. That's good news—but I still haven't found a phone and an internet connection yet. Right now we're living pretty primitively but hopefully that will change soon.

Well, I have to go now, but I'll write again soon.

Love always and forever,
J (your HUSBAND)

October 2003

Sweetie,

Today was another sad day. I helped the Chaplain with prepping for the memorial ceremony. We're going to do it on Friday. I've postponed my trip to Ramadi. We'll be very fortunate if something like this doesn't happen again before we come home. We've all been saying that it is only a matter of time. Yesterday was our time. ~ Soldier to wife

Chapter 4

The First Lines of Communication

What would military spouses do today without cell phones or Ipads? What would a military wife today do if her soldier deployed, and she didn't hear from him for six or seven weeks?

From 2001 to 2003, the Army started establishing systems for soldiers to communicate home.

There was no internet connectivity. And when the internet system was finally established, it was dial-up and spotty, and messages often got disconnected. Soldiers couldn't get home to see their babies being born. They couldn't facetime to see their new babies. They couldn't call home to wish their wife a happy birthday.

There were no cell phones. Landline was how soldiers called home. If soldiers called from a landline, they were most likely standing in a line where everyone could hear their conversations.

When they could talk, soldiers couldn't talk about where they were or what they were doing. As part of operational security, the conversation was very "muted." And while the military wife was elated that she could talk to her soldier, the conversation lacked detail and intimacy.

Telephone calls from Afghanistan or Iraq were connected to unit posts in Florida or Virginia, so if a military wife did get a call from an unknown number, for the first few times, the wife didn't answer. But when she did, a normal conversation would go like this:

"How are you doing?"-Wife

One- to two-second break. Beep.

"Fine."-Soldier

One- to two-second break. Beep.

"What have you been doing?" -Wife

One- to two-second break. Beep.

"We had a competition to see who would drink a bottle of hot sauce (or pee or some other disgusting concoction) for $20.." - Soldier

One- to two-second break. Beep.

"Why would you do that?" - Wife

One- to two-second break. Beep.

"Because we wanted to. Because soldiers are dumb." (Actual expletives deleted.) -Soldier

One- to two-second break. Beep.

"That's stupid. Well, Laguna Beach is my new favorite show. I'll write to you about the characters. I went to Target today with Caroline. And there's a red light on in the car." - Wife

One- to two-second break. Beep.

"Cool. Get the red light fixed, and don't spend all of the deployment money. That's for our vacation. I gotta go. There's a lot going on and all of these assholes want to use the phone. I love you." -Soldier

One- to two-second break. Beep.

"I love you. Be safe." - Wife

Click.

Soldiers had to take turns on the phone, sometimes standing in line for 45–50 minutes for a 5-minute conversation. They had to be quick, and God forbid the soldier show any sign of fragility. In the middle of the dry and brown desert, calling home was their 5-seconds of peace.

The USO established morale centers with landline telephones shortly after the first three years of the war. Inside the morale centers were TVs and gaming centers, free snacks and hygiene kits, and most importantly a communications center with computers and telephones.

Families sent calling cards so that soldiers, if they had time, could call their loved ones. Those calling times were unpredictable, so the military wife made sure she was always by her phone from 5 p.m. to 5 a.m. due to the time difference from the Middle East to the U.S.

After a couple of years, units were assigned two to three satellite phones per battalion. This meant that two to three phones rotated between 700 soldiers. Soldiers were very protective of their assigned times. Calls home could be scheduled and became somewhat more predictable. Soldiers would wait until the late hours at night to call home so that others couldn't hear their conversations.

Since telephone calls were sporadic, military wives hand-wrote letters. Sometimes they wrote multiple times a day to stay connected. The military wife mailed packages and became so good at completing an overseas declaration form that the mail attendants were impressed by her proficiency. She became familiar with the mail attendants.

And while writing a letter became an added routine to her weekly schedule, wives impatiently ached for word from their soldier. She timed the two weeks between letters. Some letters arrived within fourteen to sixteen days, as expected. Some took a lot longer. When day 17 arrived and there were no letters, panic set in.

Wives waited and became familiar with the mailman's routine. Sometimes letters wouldn't come, and sometimes letters would come out of sequence. Some days, there were four or five letters at once. That was the jackpot! She lived for the letters. And that's when soldiers and wives got smart about numbering letters so that the sequence of stories could be identified.

Phone calls were treasured and letters were golden. If a spouse missed a phone call because she was in the bathroom or at work or walking the dog, it ruined her whole week. She didn't know when the next call was going to come. So, she modified her schedule to be available.

So, what does a wife tell her soldier when he's deployed?

This is such an interesting question. There's the promise in all marriages that there are no secrets kept. Even white lies can eat at the soul from the inside out. But, when the soldier is deployed and has to concentrate on survival and the survival of his men, ensuring that their mental health and mindset are not inundated with the struggles from the home front is critical.

Here are some examples of stories that should and shouldn't be told:

Wife: "Honey, there's a hole in the drywall, but don't worry. I fixed it." – Yes

Wife: "Honey, there's a hole in the drywall. SOOOOO, here's what really happened. I was showing the boys that I can still do a handstand and walk on my hands. I guess my body betrayed me, and I slipped and my knee went through the wall." – NOPE! He doesn't need to know too many details.

Wife: "The boys and I are great." I got the oil changed in all of the cars. – Yes!

Wife: "The boys and I are great. I may have accidentally cut the turn too sharply at the Sonic and rubbed the side of the Suburban on the yellow pylon. Don't worry. I'll get it fixed." -No, Sir. Do NOT tell him that. It's best to just get it fixed before he gets home.

Wife: "I'm excited about our vacation when you come home. We are going to have a great vacation." -Yes.

Wife: "I've gone to see a Botox specialist. Oh, and I purchased a really expensive purse. But don't worry. There will be plenty of deployment money for a decent vacation when you get home." – NOPE!

Bottom line, there is absolutely nothing a soldier can do to help his wife when he's deployed. Too much detail about challenges at home distracts the soldier from focusing on their mission. It may also cause the soldier to feel guilty since he isn't home to help. So, the military wife learns how to be tactful about what information to share.

The stress of waiting for the call…the stress of writing letters and sending packages…and the stress of not knowing anything is how the military wife lived her life in the early days of deployment. She spent hundreds of sleepless nights just waiting for that first lines of communication.

For the mothers of soldiers

"The greatest day of my life was the day that you were born."
—Unknown

JD, Mother of Two Veteran Soldiers

There is nothing that prepares you for the love and fear you feel when you have a child.

When 9/11 happened, I was identified as my son's primary point-of-contact or the next-of-kin. I was the first identified as the first person to call in case something were to happen. The unit would send me emails about unit updates. I was the proud mother of two sons who voluntarily elected to serve in the U.S. Army.

I had a son in the 101st Airborne Division and another that was attending West Point. This was all happening at the beginning of the war. I tried to talk with my friends about my worries. While I was proud, like any mother, I was full of worry.

I would always be challenged with, "What do your sons think of the war? Why are we even there?"

My friends couldn't understand that my job as a mother was to support my sons and not necessarily to discuss the war. I always mentioned that my sons didn't really have an opinion . . . they just supported our country and its leadership. And so, I really had no one at home to talk with about my boys. I found that my support came from other West Point parents and the military community. They understood the everyday sinking feeling and fear.

My boys were very different. I would describe one as kind and the other as quiet.

From 2001, I would obsess about watching the news. As a mother, we are trained to grab the boys if they fell out of the boat. I couldn't grab my boys, so I did the next best thing . . . I did as much research as I could.

I kept scrapbooks, took notes. I kept a log of their history as soldiers. I followed their every mission.

And then I got the worst call ever: Your son is injured and he's being shipped to Walter Reed.

It was 2007, and my son was in Ramadi. The nurses called me immediately. It was my worst nightmare.

Every American citizen should have to tour Walter Reed at one point of their lives to see our soldiers. When my son was injured in Ramadi, he was shipped to Walter Reed. My heart broke. We were lucky, the Army took care of us with a food and housing allowance.

I was only the mother of one injured son, but I wish I could have been the mother to all of the soldiers there.

Most of the boys wanted to go back to their units. When our son was able to go home, we took him home to Kansas. He was in a wheelchair for three months. He was angry. And he felt no different than the boys did at Walter Reed. He was ready to get back to his soldiers and the unit. He was not happy to be at home with his mama.

And just like that, my heart broke all over again.

Chapter 5

Stand By

"Stand by" is a phrase often used by the military to tell the soldier to "hold on" or "wait." It's kind of a brash way of saying, "Please wait. I'll be with you when I'm ready."

The Army often uses this phrase to tell the soldiers to wait and to be ready to move.

And for a mother of a military soldier, *standing by* is the hardest thing she has to do.

Mother: she is typically a baby's first source of comfort. She's the first person to hold, feed, and bathe her baby. She holds his hand to cross the street; she teaches him right from wrong.

When a mother surrenders responsibility of her child to the Army, all she can do is stand by and pray. Proud and honored. She raised a man who has chosen a life of service.

If her son isn't married, she is identified as the next-of-kin. She's given information about field exercises and deployments. She is first to be informed if the soldier is hurt, wounded, or killed in action. Unfortunately, this dynamic changes when a soldier is married. When a soldier marries, all that the mother can do is *stand by* and WAIT.

When a soldier identifies his wife as the primary next-of-kin, all information regarding the soldier is communicated with the wife. The military has no obligation to notify the parents. While this is understood, this is also a dagger to every mother's heart. All she can do is wait for someone to call her and give her information.

The soldier's spouse is relayed information about deployment and if a soldier is wounded or killed in action. It is the spouse who has to relay the information to the soldier's mother. And throughout the deployment, all the mother can do is stand by and wait. She's on the sidelines just waiting.

She wakes in the morning and turns on the news. She turns on the computer after she pours her cup of coffee and spends the day doing research. She researches every article published about the war, HOPING not to hear anything about her soldier—her son.

She's learned intimate details about her son's unit and where they are going. She's learned the unit motto and the unit chain of command. She's learned to be patient.

But all she can do is stand by.

Throughout the six-, nine-, twelve-, or fifteen-month deployments, all she can do is send her love with no expectation of hearing anything. She sends packages and cards, with the hopes that they are received. She prays that she receives a call or letter. She waits.

And then God forbid tragedy happens, and her son is wounded or, worst yet, killed in action. A mother is NOT the first to be notified. A mother has to stand by and wait. She has to wait until the wife is notified. She just stands by. And she waits.

She's no longer the source of comfort. She can no longer hold his hand. She can't tell him he's right for fighting everything that is wrong. She just stands by.

For all the mothers out there, standing by and waiting, may God give you comfort and strength. For the military wives, athlete wives, first-responder wives, wives whose partners work long hours, leaving you for hours and days and months at a time, and those who are carrying the weight of the world on their shoulders . . .you are the rocks and the glue that allow them to succeed.

Thank you for standing by. Thank you for always being there... waiting.

"Some days you will feel like the ocean. Some days you will feel like you are drowning in it."

—Lori Mathis

"I've read all of the parenting books, cook books, and coaching books. I'm overloaded by life, so I've perfected how to compartmentalize my emotions and feelings and my thoughts so that I don't completely lose my shit. I'm a mom; I am their protector. I have to be sweet and compassionate, but also stern. I'm a dad; I'm the disciplinarian and their coach; I have to be strict but fair. I have to teach the boys how to be gentlemen without losing sight of their childhood. How do I get from one day to the next?"

—Military Wife

There are days where I've proclaimed, "I quit parenting! The hours are too fucking long, and the pay just sucks."

—Military wife

Apparently, my threats are empty, and I'm barely holding on. I've used the following choice phrases toward my kids:

I'm calling the MPs (military police) because you are safer with me behind bars.

I'm going to shave your eyebrows when you are sleeping. Actually, I'm going to shave just one so that YOU have to shave the other one.

If you don't pick up your room and laundry, I will throw your laundry into the snow.

What do you mean you don't eat Great Value chips?! Then eat air!

—Military Wife

Chapter 6

Overloaded

Ellen Degeneres. What can I say about Ellen? She was there in 2005 on the television set in the birthing room when I delivered my first child. She made me laugh, and my husband knew that I needed something to distract me from the pain that I was feeling.

She was there in 2006, when I said good-bye to my soldier before he deployed. I got home from the farewell, and I turned her show on. She reminded me that life is simple and happy and everything was going to be ok.

Ellen was there in 2010 when I was having trouble with yet another deployment and angry spouses. Her last lines of the day resonated with me when she said, "be kind to one another." And that message is one that I live with every day!

I was actually Ellen for Halloween in 2019. People were like: who are you? And I responded with a huff, "Ellen. Can't you tell?!"

Throughout the years, she had done multiple military reunions and gave generous gifts because I believe that it brought her joy. Her sincere generosity gave me hope in humanity and how a little appreciation can wash away anything ugly in the world.

For almost 20-years, Ellen has been a part of my life. For that short hour every day, she relieved any burden I was carrying. While Ellen was on, I never felt overloaded.

Congratulations on being married to a soldier. Your life is going to be everything you NEVER imagined.

First, it's going to be full of stress and uncertainty ALL THE TIME. If you have any career ambitions, you might want to reconsider them because chances are, you're going to be moving every three to four years. Oh! And as your soldier continues to get promoted, you're probably going to have to move every two to three years. So, if you have any training or an advanced degree that requires licensure for currency, guess what? You're going to have to either take an exam or pay for licensure for EVERY state you move to if you want to work. Oh . . . and by the time you take the exam and apply for employment, chances are, it's time to move AGAIN.

Secondly, find a good hobby to occupy your time because you are going to be alone a lot. Make sure that you learn how to handle all of the household responsibilities. Yes, you are responsible for anything that is going on in the house. Your soldier's schedule is from 0600 to about 1900 hours. That's on average. Sometimes there's training that will be over the weekends. Don't be disappointed...just get used to it.

Now let's discuss visiting exotic places. Yes! You'll probably get one cool duty station: Hawaii or Korea or Japan or Europe. That's only if your soldier is SUPER lucky. But there's a very good chance you will end up in Louisiana, North Dakota, the desert of California, or the frozen tundra in Alaska or Upstate New York. Try to find the good in all of the new places you are lucky to see. Chances are you will have to stay a lot longer in a place that you hate.

There's some voluntary military spouse training available, if you want to take it...the classes will teach you about rank and post programs. What it won't teach you is how to really survive this life.

Remember, you shouldn't rely on your soldier for anything because their #1 priority is their job with the military.

Welcome to the military, and good luck with being a military wife. Your adventure is just beginning."

Signed,
Military Leaders

There are very few professions that compare to the stress of military life: athlete families, first responders, and single parents. The stress level of the wife is comparable to that of her husband's. While he prepares to compete in his game, or goes to war, or gets called to respond to an emergency, the wife is overloaded with the stress of handling the home and the discipline and safety of her children.

There are days when the weight of the world is on her shoulders. She wants to scream, kick, punch, and scream more. She wants to break things. She wants to break lots of things. And then there are days where she's so overloaded with the burden of dealing with everyday life by herself that she wants to run away and sit on the beach with a cocktail.

For the military wife, there's no better training on resiliency than adversity. Adversity seems to surface every time a soldier is gone. She actually becomes quite good at "dealing with it."

She can't tell her soldier that the car tire is flat while he's in the field, so she deals with it. She also can't tell the soldier that she lost her debit card and someone has stolen her identity, so she deals with it.

What does she do in this scenario: They just moved to Colorado and she knows no one. Her family is in Maryland, and she has three children under the age of seven. Her soldier deploys 5-weeks after moving to Colorado. They are still moving into their house, so they haven't really met anyone, and it's November. Her two-year old child is sick in the middle of the night, and she has to go to the hospital. Does she knock on the neighbor's door at 2:37 AM to ask for help to watch the other two children or does she take all three with her to the hospital?

The two-year-old is throwing-up in the car, and now all three children are screaming and crying. She somehow makes it to the hospital emergency room with a puke-smelled car, and all three children are still screaming and crying. She carries the baby in while the other two dawdle behind her with their blankets, and she waits to be checked in.

The doctor informs her that the baby has to be checked into the hospital for observation. What does she do? Who does she call? How can she check in the baby and stay with the baby, and she has two other children?

She only knows the name of her husband's unit. She only knows he's deployed and she's in Colorado. She calls her mother crying. She's overloaded.

Although she believes she can handle the military life by herself, it's emergency situations like this that makes the military wife realize that she must trust a the new unit and the spouses that are in it. She must trust the other wives quickly, even though she doesn't know them, she has to let her guard down.

She must be willing to swallow her pride and expose her vulnerability, even though her entire life, she's been taught that exposing her vulnerability is a sign of weakness. She learns quickly that she has to find an emergency contact person every time she moves. And while she knows that finding this person is crucial to hers and her family's survival, she has to be willing to reciprocate the assistance.

In the military culture, the military wife quickly learns that she is not a single-unit, but rather a rivet helping to keep the Army machine operating. And so, she learns that being overloaded is a part of military life, but there are other wives that will help her if she asks. In return, she accepts the responsibility of helping others, as well.

This is how the military wife survived the war. She created pods of support every time she moved because she learned that the village-mentality is what helped them all survive even the worst of scenarios. She needed help to keep from being overloaded.

Ellen, would've been a great military spouse. Whether she knows it or not, she was a member of my support pod. Thank you, Ellen, for bringing me joy every day. Thank you for making me laugh in times when I could've cried all day. Thank you for teaching me that love and kindness are to be given to everyone. And thank you for keeping me from always being overloaded.

2005–2009

March 9, 2006

It's early on the eve of your departure. Our farewell was very different from the last time—we said goodbyes in our car. That goodbye was nothing like before. You're a leader now, and I think we both understand that it's important for you to be strong.

We held our eight-month-old son and cried. He couldn't quite comprehend what was going on, but he could definitely tell we were both sad. So, all three of us had a good cry. Right now, our son is watching videos, and I'm frantically checking to see if you had forgotten anything. Do you remember that from the last deployment?

Leave. Come home. Leave. Come home.

I'm starting to feel sad, honey. I know this day is tough for both of us, but I want you to know that WE can handle it. Although you can't be here for his first birthday, he won't remember it. I'm lucky you were here to watch him grow, and I'm very lucky to have you as a husband and a father to our son. I love you, and I miss you more than you will ever know. God protect and keep you. Do your best to bring ALL our boys home - Military wife.

March 10, 2006

I haven't been happy all day. I came home from playgroup, took a nap, and snuggled with our son and rode out the horrible thunderstorm. The cable still isn't working, and I'm not very motivated to do anything right now. So you can only imagine how lonely it feels not having you here to hang out with.

I will send the (Joneses) family flowers. Bless their hearts. How tragic! How's Lt. Jones doing? I can't believe that just hours before deployment, he kissed his mother, grandparents, and sister goodbye. As they were driving home, there was a car accident. Everyone but his mama was killed in a car crash! My aching heart. His poor grandparents and little sister.

I will send flowers and see if Ms. Jones needs anything. I'll be sure to check in with the chaplain and Lt. Jones as well since he's still here.

I love you. I miss you. Tomorrow will be a better day.

-Military wife

Chapter 7

The Two-Front War

A two-front war occurs when enemy forces encounter one another on separate fronts. From 2005 to 2008, the two-front war in the Middle East happened overseas *and* at home.

Soldiers, our heroes, were home and then gone again, and then home again and then GONE again. Their minds didn't have time to settle down when they were home. Soldiers were still running on the adrenaline from the deployment. Unfortunately, in the wake of deployment is the military wife and the family.

GWOT military wives became experts on knowing the deployment process. This—only four or five years after the war had begun. Just as quickly as soldiers were home, they were leaving again. The military wife became an expert in knowing the deployment rotational sequence. She became increasingly confident in her ability to remain calm and operate independently. Where she did struggle was during the redeployment and reintegration phase.

The military started to identify the growing level of mental strain placed on soldiers and their families came as a result of multiple deployments and long periods of separation. Systems were put in place to measure deployment stress on soldiers prior to redeployment as a preventative.

What was the Army trying to prevent?

In August 2005, Military Medicine published a "Post-deployment domestic violence by U.S. Army soldiers" article. This and many succeeding articles brought heightened national awareness to the predictability of domestic violence on wives of soldiers who had participated in a six-month or longer deployment. Military leaders were asked to head caution when a soldier came home.

The Army Chaplain Corps started allocating funds for marriage retreats to assist with the reintegration of the soldier into the family. While the theory was optimistic, this was a voluntary program that had limited funding, so only a few families/couples were selected to attend.

So, while the soldier had a difficult time adjusting to the role of husband or father from being a warrior soldier, the military wife and the children had an equally difficult time adjusting to the soldier being home. Herein lies the two-front war.

While the nation became hyper-focused on the mental health of the soldiers before, during, and after redeployment, it wasn't until 2017 that the Department of Defense identified that there was a correlation with deployments, the uncertainty of day-to-day scheduling, and moving to multiple duty stations that directly lead to high rates of stress, anxiety, depression, sleeplessness, and unemployment with military spouses.

In the early stages of the war, there was still a stigma with seeing a mental health counselor. There was some misconception that if a wife sought counseling, her husband's chain of command would be notified and that somehow, her mental health could affect his career. If the soldier saw a counselor, then he would be identified as unfit to deploy or a detriment to mission readiness.

Basically, there was this unfounded belief that if the wife had a mental health issue, the soldier's home life was unstable. This meant that the soldier couldn't properly focus on the mission. And the ripple effect meant that the soldier was unfit to deploy and at-risk for promotional consideration.

All of these allegations were unfounded, but in the early days of deployment, the two-front war was being fought at home and overseas. And occasionally, a battle was lost.

Since there was a negative stigma associated with mental health counseling, the military wife became an expert at suppressing her emotions. She didn't want to be identified as a mental health concern. So how did she cope? How did she handle her mental health stress? How did she prepare for the reintegration of her soldier after being separated for six to eighteen months?

She called her military sisters for counsel. This support network was critical to keeping the military spouse mentally sane.

She learned how to cope with day-to-day deployment challenges and reintegration preparation. Some spouses chose church or exercise or found a hobby. Other wives sought professional therapy. Depression, anxiety, and sleeplessness were very real diagnosis and needed professional attention.

Sometimes, the military wife's prescription for coping would look like this:

Sleepless nights:

Call a military sister!

> Red wine – for those light nights when she's up until 12 a.m.
> Vodka – for those nights when she's up until 2 a.m.

> Ambien – for those nights when she can't sleep

Anxiety:

Call a military sister!

> Exercise: walking, riding a bike, or running

> Klonopin: for when the days are intolerable and she's hypersensitive

***Alcohol is a horrible way to treat anxiety, but in case of an emergency, Tequila helps tremendously

Depression:

Call a military sister!

> Request a happy hour, karaoke night with said military sisters with whatever mix of seasonal drinks.

> Lexapro, Prozac, Zoloft – take your pick. For when it's hard to get out of bed, go grocery shopping or take care of the family.

Stress:

Call a military sister!

Find a workout class like yoga, cycling, or boot camp if you have time; walk around the block.

Wine! LOTS OF IT

These solutions may not be ideal for dealing with stress or deployments, but the two-front war for the military spouse became a trial-and-error scenario.

While her soldier prepared to come home, the military wife prepared herself for him to be home. How do you allow a person to reintegrate into a life when you've been operating on auto-drive without him?

For years, the military wife has had to live vigilantly. Her life revolved around the life or death of soldiers every day. She constantly lived on a high sense of alert. She was always worried that she was going to get "the" call or "the visit" and needed to be ready if she did. But what would she do if she or her friend got "the" call or "the visit?" Then what?

Taking it "easy" wasn't in her vocabulary.

So, the conversations of finding balance in a home and battling the mental health and stability for both the soldier and the wife started to surface. The military medical community started to give greater attention to researching methods to help the soldier, the spouse, and the children. Mental health specialists advocated that counseling wasn't a stigma but a necessity for reintegration. They advocated that counseling would assist in preventing alcohol and stimulant abuse amongst the military spouse community. They advocated that military children required counseling in order to adjust to having the soldier's presence back in the family.

The two-front mental health war started to bubble to the surface in the military community. Leaders were finally recognizing the toll that deployments and reintegration were taking on soldiers and their families. Physical abuse and divorce statistics were at an all-time high in the military, and military wives were becoming increasingly impatient

51

with the military support system. Leaders were beginning to recognize that reintegration wasn't an easy process.

For as long as the U.S. military existed, the military organization always expected that military wives would handle the stress of operating a household independently. But then there was also the expectation that she would seamlessly welcome the soldier's authority back into her solo operational system immediately upon redeployment. In many cases, this was not the truth.

Reintegration was not as simple as turning a light switch on and off. Unfortunately, that is what a soldier's presence at home felt like. They were home and they were gone. And the military wife, after placing single parent systems in place while the soldier was gone, was expected to easily share those responsibilities upon his return. The transition was never that easy.

Leaders were now forced to address this epidemic and consider developing better reintegration systems for both the soldier and the family. What leaders were facing at this stage of the war was longer and more stressful reintegration periods, and a growing population of unhappy spouses who had grown accustomed to operating a home without her soldier.

And as painful as it was for the the military spouse to admit, she became "ok" with her soldier deploying again. This was just the beginning of the two-front mental health war. Soldiers started to accept that they were always deploying and that their presence and authority at home was temporary. Military wives started to redefine what a healthy, functioning military family looked like as they normalized deployments into their everyday lives.

2010–2013

10 Years and Still at War

"To me, having him gone was normal. I knew how to operate without him." -Military wife

Chapter 8

Normal

What is the normal amount of black leggings a woman should own? This is a legitimate question. My mother came to visit me while my husband was deployed. I was happy to have her help with the kids, but my mother is a very old school and proper woman. She believed that women should always be poised and presentable in public. She especially detested leggings in public. One of our conversations looked something like this:

"Don't you have a meeting today?"-Mom

"Yes, mom. Thanks for helping with the kids."-Me

"Why are you wearing leggings?"-Mom

"They're black leggings. And these aren't just leggings. These are nice ones." -Me

"Honey, there is no such thing as nice leggings. Unless you are planning on going to the gym afterwards, you can at least put some slacks on. They have stretchy pants if you want to wear something like leggings. But, wearing leggings to a meeting screams that you are lazy. Oh…and please put some mascara and lipstick on. You look haggard. Don't give anyone the impression that you can't handle your life."-Mom

I was infuriated with her. How dare she judge me. How dare she say that I can't handle my life. But while staring at my reflection in the mirror, I realized that she may have had a point. Somewhere in the last 10-years, I had become lazy. I owned 9-pairs of black leggings because that was the easy solution to dressing every day, and I made the black legging my normal uniform. I owned capri cut-black leggings, full length-black

56

leggings, fancy speckled-black leggings, and multiple different brand black leggings that somehow all looked the exact same. At that moment in time, I realized that I had changed so much in 10-years of being married, military wife. Somewhere between the first deployment and 10-years, I had lost my sense of self and I was looking for the easy solution.

The military had changed significantly since the first stages of the war. Cell phones were available now, so communication was frequent. Deployments still came with heightened emotional and mental anxiety, but they were a little more predictable. The family unit became comfortable operating without their soldier. And they accepted deployments as *normal.*

The deployment farewells were less dramatic. There were still staging areas, but military wives practically did a drive-by and drop-off. Some soldiers would drive themselves to work and just requested that the wife pick-up their vehicles at the unit area. This was also considered a normal farewell.

The GWOT children were getting older. Parents started to rewrite the narrative: Daddy was going to "help the good guys learn how to fight the bad guys." And while the reality of "losing daddy" was still very real, the soldier leaving the house was considered normal.

The military wife had become familiar with the military language. She knew policies. And since her nomadic life often prevented her from being able to find stable employment, she operated the home like her own business and she was the CEO. Routines were put in place. And she took on the responsibility of mentoring young spouses on how to survive the military life. In her calendar, she penciled in phone dates with her soldier. They were predictable and frequent. And with video chat, she could actually see her soldier's face.

She was ready.

She was prepared to handle being a single parent. She was prepared to work with young military spouses and encourage them to stay strong. She accepted her role: military wife and leader. This was her new definition of normal.

She was prepared this time . . . in case she got the call or a visit. She was pragmatic about deployments. She knew that her soldier's job was dangerous, but she was prepared for the worst.

It's hard to fathom, but the military wife was comfortable with deployments and her soldier's lack of presence. She knew exactly how to live a life without her soldier. She became emotionally numb to all of the stressors because, quite honestly, she had survived the early phase of the war where communication support systems were non-existent.

In 2010, military funded programs implemented tons of resources to help the military wife and family with deployment stress. There was no longer a stigma with asking for mental health support.

Survival was essential, and the military spouse depended on all resources for support. She asked for help if she needed it. She was happy to offer help if it was needed, as well. At this stage, the ten-year mark into the war, the military spouse was no longer "that" worried. Operating without her soldier was NORMAL. It was HER normal life.

While admitting that my mother was right is like drinking vinegar water, she had a point. I had made taking the easy way out NORMAL. Somewhere along the way, I had lost myself, my dignity, my drive to fight, and I had purchased 9-pairs of black leggings. I had given up on myself and surrendered to taking it easy.

At that moment in time, she made me realize that life is hard. Living a military life is very hard. I had made concessions and chose to just cope instead of fight.

In the great card game of life, being a military wife was the hand that I was dealt. I could either play the game or I could fold before the game even starts. Either way, I needed to put my poker face on and fight. And I needed to play the game and not take the easy way out because that was cheating.

I realized that I needed to fight every day to fit into my slacks. I needed to be proud and have some self-worth. I needed to put my red lipstick and mascara on and start each day with a fresh face. Because I was a professional military wife and I was going to work. I shouldn't wear leggings to the grocery store or to a meeting or just out unless I was going to the gym or coming from the gym. I needed to approach each day as an opportunity to inspire and mentor young military spouses to fight. I needed to elect to wear pants or a dress because opting to wear just black leggings symbolized that I was surrendering to taking the easy way out every day. And, my black leggings should be a "treat" instead of just normal wear.

It was at that moment with mama that I realized that the rest of the world, just like me, was fighting to make every day count. And it's the fight for survive that is NORMAL. And I needed to give the impression that I can handle it.

Chapter 9

Stand there and look pretty

Trophy wife. There are many theories on the origin of the term, but the derogatory implications that a wife has little personal merit but her physical attractiveness is the same. The term further eludes that a wife spends substantial money on her appearance is unintelligent and has little substance.

While the military wife is never formerly told that she is always being watched, the military culture, unlike any profession, has many expectations of the spouse and her family. Some would even argue that her unofficial OFFICIAL job, in addition to maintaining the house, volunteering at the unit, and possibly maintaining a job, is to "stand there and look pretty" like a trophy wife.

The military is a culture where a soldier's family member could positively and adversely affect his career. Soldiers are in the business where they must be ALWAYS mission ready. Ready to train, fight, and deploy. If a soldier is distracted by household stressors, then can he be reliable to handle the stressors of his mission?

There's no basic training to teach the spouse about what her role may be in the relationship. There are many traditional social events in the military. There are casual events like unit functions to more formal events like balls or VIP dinners. The unspoken expectation is that the military spouse will be charming, presentable, and a representative of her spouse and his unit. She is supposed to just STAND THERE AND LOOK PRETTY.

It's only through mentorship and years of learning from role models that the military spouse understands that she is to represent her spouse with grace and poise. STAND THERE AND LOOK PRETTY.

During the GWOT era, military spouses were now being captured by the media. Not only were they being photographed, but they are now being interviewed. The media was relentless about interviewing a spouse anywhere at any time. And what the media often portrayed was the young military wife, in pajama pants and her husband's unit shirt at the Wal-Mart with two screaming kids and a haggard face. What the media didn't portray until years later were the thousands of hours that spouses volunteered for the military.

Military wives were the primary advocates soliciting donations to prepare the soldiers barracks for redeployment. They coordinated fundraisers and asked for corporate donations so that funding was available for a unit ball. Military spouses attended meetings with legislators to advocate for military family well-being.

The military wife was expected and encouraged to volunteer, manage a home, balance a job, and cope with a deployment without any formal training or financial compensation. On top of all of those responsibilities, she was expected to STAND THERE AND LOOK PRETTY.

There are so many ripple effects of the military spouse's discourse that can affect the entire functioning of the military and the unit. If the military spouse talked openly or published something with negative undertones about the unit and the soldier's well-being to the media, senior leaders were immediately involved. The unit leadership would be investigated for toxicity. The soldier's household would be investigated for validity of the spouse's allegations. For as many responsibilities she was given, regardless of how much grief and angst she felt, she was just expected to STAND THERE AND LOOK PRETTY.

The military spouse is never formally told that she can positively AND negatively affect the military, the unit, and soldier. Nor is she told that she can positively AND negatively affect mission readiness. That she plays a powerful role in the success and the failure of the unit and the family. She is essentially the modern day Helen of Troy affecting the temperament of a country: the military. There are very few, if any, careers where the military spouse and the family can affect a soldier's career spectacularly.

After 10-years of war, the military finally recognized that the military spouse played a vital role in information dissemination to families, especially younger military wives. So, senior/seasoned military wives were encouraged to volunteer to be a part of the unit information distribution system. They were encouraged to be role models. They were encouraged to inspire other military wives to volunteer, learn the military culture so that the soldier can focus on his mission, and to perfect how to best represent the military, the unit and the soldier by STANDING THERE AND LOOKING PRETTY.

Overall, the military expects that the military wife to adopt the "no one wants to see your dirty laundry" concept. She is responsible for the housekeeping and the drama of the home. She is expected to keep all of the drama and dirty laundry at home so that the soldier can be mission ready.

Fortunately for the military, majority of military spouses are poised, beautiful, and committed. They can handle the household, the unit expectations, a part-time job, a full-time job, volunteer requirements, and changing a tire. They can do all of that, and STAND THERE AND LOOK PRETTY.

Dan and Allie: There's a Silver Lining at the End of Every Storm

Dan's Story, 2011

Email from Paula to Dan:

Since I was online today, I looked at divorce paperwork. Check out complete casecase.com. See if it's legit. $299 plus court fee of $100 or so.

-Paula, 2011

Email from sister to Dan:

> *Wow! I'm speechless. I'm not being ugly . . . well, shit! Yes, I am. Are you freakin' kidding me? Online divorce?! Is it that important for her to have this separation complete before you even get home from deployment?*

> *The least she could do is wait for you so that together you can talk to the kids. Honestly, this whole thing is selfish. She's totally not thinking about emotionally scarring the boys. I want to kick her in her VAGINA. YES, I'm angry.*

> *Brother, I love you. Stay focused! Hang in there, and get home safely. Everyone goes through something or another during their relationship. But this is unbelievable.*

> *I know that I'm not helping you, but what makes me upset is the way she's handling it. I'LL ONLINE DROP KICK HER IN HER THROAT IF SHE DOESN'T START SHOWING SOME COMPASSION.*

Keep your head up and your spirits high. I'm sorry I got a little angry. You know me.

Love you, Big Brother,

-R, 2011

Email from Dan to sister:

I told Paula to research about the divorce if that was her will. It truly shows what she wants to do. The truth is, she had been planning this process for years. She waited until I was deployed to push for it.

The boys don't know anything yet as she says, but me and the boys have a connection that is so tight I feel they know something. Michael already told his Mom he will never leave me. Terence will just follow his big brother.

We had a discussion on how things will play out. Paula said the house, my retirement, and all belongings in the house are mine. We are going to split the checking/savings and mutual funds. We have our own retirement funds. The boys will stay with me. She said once she settles in Florida she wants the boys to at least start a semester with her next year.

She said all she's leaving with is her car, her clothes and her coffee machine. So you can see, she just wants out.

I love you, Sis.

-Dan, 2011

Allie's Story

At one point in my life, I accepted that this was my career now. And after serving as an Army officer on active duty, I took on the greatest career challenge of my life: being married to an infantry soldier who deployed and the mother of two special-needs children. I had accepted the fact that my job was taking care of my family.

What I didn't know was that I was going to be in a very lonely marriage.

He was always gone. Even when he wasn't deployed and he was home, he was still not present.

I used to resent other soldiers who walked their kids to school holding their wife's hand. I used to believe that "that soldier doesn't work as hard as mine."

And after a while, I no longer believed that. I started to see it very differently. I started to feel like "I" was not a priority. I mentioned this to my husband, and I asked, actually pleaded for him to make me and the kids first. I needed help.

For years into the marriage, he still never attended an appointment with me. I remember having to medically transport our daughter because she was having seizures, and he didn't leave the field to help me.

His actions didn't make me feel like I was first.

He once volunteered to take the kids to an appointment. But, like always, he changed the plans and I still ended up going by myself.

So, fast forward sixteen years into a marriage where I resented him, I tried to force my feelings. I forced myself to feel love. I forced myself to want to have sex. I was empty. But I wanted this to work for our children.

You know, he had a ton of vacation leave built up, since he was gone all the time. Instead of planning a family vacation for our three children and me, he would go hunting for two to three weeks. He wanted to go on a trip. He needed a vacation from the Army. He needed a vacation from his family.

I was still left all alone with the children—with no help.

I knew our relationship had ended when he told me he had to "mentally" prepare for family dinners because they were too chaotic. He clearly didn't want to be around us, and I no longer wanted to be around him.

We just couldn't figure it out, although, to the military world, we were a successful couple. I was the stay-at-home wife who took care of everything. He was the multi-deployed hero.

I just couldn't keep doing it alone. I needed help. I needed a partner. I wanted love. And so, I quit.

Chapter 10

Dear John

What's the point of being married if I'm alone all of the time?
—Military Wife, 2021

That's a valid question. What *is* the point of being married if you are alone all of the time?

God, country, corps. This mantra is what separates the military career from many other professions, When soldiers voluntarily commits his life to defending our nation, he also commits the lives of his family's. This is not to say that the soldier isn't devoted to his ife and family. It basically means that the sacrifice of a soldier's service is also the sacrifice of a wife's life and that of their children.

There's a cynical joke about Marine soldiers being married: *If the Corps wanted the soldier to have a wife, they would have issued him one.*

Most people don't enter into a marriage telling themselves, "I can't wait to marry you and spend the majority of this life alone," or "I can't wait to get married and be a single parent" or "I hope that this marriage is exciting and full of stress."

Like many relationships, couples fall in love. They marry because they want to grow together. They marry because they are partners ready to take on the challenges of the world together.

Unfortunately for the military wife, she's never told that the relationship growth with her soldier isn't like that of a traditional marriage.

This was definitely the ugly truth for military couples of the GWOT generation. The GWOT generation military couple DOES NOT grow "together."

For the GWOT generation couple, they learned to grow side-by-side with the occasional intersection of circles.

The military is an honorable profession that provides life support services to a family. The military lifestyle is often regarded as a security blanket for many families. It's easy to feel safe with healthcare, life insurance, and dental insurance. While some would consider this as lucky, the unreasonable cost is a soldier's time and life. The soldier spends twelve- to fifteen-hour days working toward mission success and combat readiness. And the military wife operated in her 10-to-12-hour circle separately.

It's very easy to fall in love with a soldier: handsome, fit, smart. And even if she initially took a vow that everything in her marriage would be equal, that doesn't apply to the military wife. The military wife is alone all of the time, so she has had to redefine her ideals about the "perfect marriage."

And what it boils down to is this: marriage is work. It's especially hard work in a military marriage. It takes commitment by both parties and an understanding that the military wife, her career, her goals, and her idea of an egalitarian marriage play secondary to the career of the soldier and his commitment to the security of our nation. And if it is not outlined in the beginning stages of a military marriage that the soldier's commitment to his military career often takes precedence over the family, the relationship will grow roots of resentment and discourse.

In a military relationship, plans change often and promises are often broken. For example: a soldier is supposed to be home from the field on Wednesday, the day before his wife's birthday. Another soldier in the unit loses his night vision goggle in the field, and so now, the field exercise has been extended until Saturday. The soldier is now missing his wife's birthday. What can she do about this? Is she upset? Naturally. But, can she change the outcome of this scenario? No.

In 2010, Lasse Hallstrom directed the romantic war drama film Dear John based on the Nicholas Sparks novel. If anyone has seen the film, the story follows a young soldier who falls in love with a college student. At the height of their romance, he's notified that he is deploying, and they commit to staying connected via letters. Their story starts in 2001 . . .

To a military wife, the movie's entire storyline can be painfully accurate. Nicholas Sparks portrayed the emotional hardship of love and separation. Time, space, uncertainty, lack of communication, pain, and loneliness are factors that result in a dangerous equation. And when there is shaky ground in a relationship, promises are broken. When John extends to stay another tour in Afghanistan, Savannah feels betrayed because he initially committed to getting out of the Army and coming home.

As time passes, Savannah's letters become less frequent. She starts to resent John, until she finally gives up and sends her "Dear John" letter.

In 2012, Dan received an email from his wife that she wanted a divorce. He was deployed to Iraq, helping support the efforts to decrease U.S. forces and reallocate equipment. They got married when they were in their early twenties in 1995, and remained married for fourteen years.

Separation, having children, and growing older affected their relationship. This is true for Dan and Paula. As a young military wife, the adventures of moving and seeing the world were exciting. But, as time went on, she realized that she no longer wanted the military life. She wanted a companion and affection, and Dan wasn't there. Paula did not want to be alone. Paula did not want this marriage. She did not want to be a military wife.

She found comfort with a man that was NOT deployed. She had an affair with a man that filled her loneliness. And in a way that may seem unforgiveable to some, she sent Dan an email asking him for a divorce while Dan was deployed.

She was a lonely woman, exhausted and aching for attention. It was easy for Paula to scheme leaving Dan while he was deployed. Actually, it was Dan's deployments that solidified her decision that she no longer wanted to be married . . . that the military life was not for her, and that her definition of marriage did not match his.

Unfortunately, her anxiousness led to impatience. She emailed a divorce-filing website to Dan. This was her "Dear John" letter when he was deployed. It was easy for her to be courageous when he was not there. Their story is not unique to the military.

Throughout the war, there were many stories like this. The story line isn't exact, but military spouses struggled. They struggled being alone. She struggled with constant change and the uncertainty of the future. They struggled with the dark cloud of death looming overhead every day. And as the military wife began to create a life without her soldier, that life became normal.

Wives were alone all of the time and there was no end in sight. The military never released information about when the war was going to end because the truth is, they didn't know. And military wives didn't know HOW long they were going to be alone.

From 2010 to 2013, the military started to see an increase of military divorce rates. Separation and deployments were factors that may have influenced these decisions.

The wife had to decide if the military life and the lack of time and help from her soldier were enough. Is a life of constant worry what she wanted? Is that life what she signed up for when she got married to a soldier?

Annie's story is very different. After twenty years of hard work trying to maintain a relationship, she finally had the epiphany: my soldier is unwilling to change for his family, so I am no longer willing to make any more sacrifices.

Sometimes things just don't work out.....that is true for any relationship. The military life demands a lot from military spouses. If there isn't a compromise and understanding between the soldier and his spouse about the demands and expectations, then the couple will struggle to find harmony and happiness.

For Annie, it was very difficult for her soldier to turn off the Army and deployment modes. What she identified after 20-years of marriage is her soldier's inability to disconnect from the military when he was at home. This tainted the relationship with the family. And as his career progressed and his responsibilities became greater with every promotion, her soldier became less available to the family and his wife.

Her soldier was physically present, but always connected to work. And she found that there was no cooperation. She was expected to handle anything at home by herself.

How patient does a military wife need to be? Were her personal and professional goals important? What happened to her affectionate, patient, caring, thoughtful husband? How many times does a wife need to ask her husband to be present? For Annie, 20-years of sacrifice made the decision to leave a lot easier than staying in an unappreciative relationship.

Soldiers, in some instances, may have been physically present for their families, but many were emotional and mental unavailable. And when a soldier isn't present for the wife to grow with, that need for connection is found elsewhere.

The military wife is strained by the constant loom of uncertainty and loneliness. It's often difficult to find a silver lining in a life where the dark cloud of fear is always evident. Every day, when her soldier is gone for training or deployment, there is the fear of death. And that fear is what separates the military life from any other career.

Leaning on other military spouses to maneuver through the day-to-day challenges helps. But if she doesn't choose to change her ideas about a successful military marriage, chances are, she may find herself just another Savannah sending her Dear John letter.

For the service members away from home on the holidays

"Lord, won't you give me the strength to make it through somehow. I've never been more homesick than now."
~unknown

"The house is decorated. Check. The cookies are being made. Check. Christmas cards . . . do I do those this year?"
—Military Wife

"It's so hard to be joyful when the half of me is gone. I dread the months from October to January....because chances are, my soldier is either deployed or training to deploy."
—Military Wife

"I ugly cry in the shower, especially around the holidays. The shower is actually the best place to cry, anyway. I can ugly-cry in the shower and no one will hear me. Plus, I'm already wet, so it's a win–win.

-Military Wife

"I make all of his favorites; cookies, dinner. But somehow, that makes me miss him more. I send presents overseas so he has something to open like us. But on the morning of Christmas, I wake earlier than everyone. I have my coffee, and I sit in his chair, and I allow myself to cry so that the kids don't see me. And then I muscle-up all of my energy to be happy."
—Military Wife

Chapter 11

Holiday Blues

The holidays worldwide are a time of joy. Even on Christmas Day in 1914, soldiers from the Royal British Army, German, and French Armies ceased fire and crossed the trenches to exchange Christmas greetings. On that Christmas Day, soldiers paused from attacking one another and played a game of soccer. There was joy.

In 2014, 100 years after the great war, Sainsbury's grocery store released a commercial depicting this cease-fire and the very act of holiday unity. It was such an amazing video. It showed how, on Christmas Day, soldiers can set aside their differences and celebrate life.

Now, soldiers are fighting a war where religious beliefs are very different and where the ideals of peace are a foreign idea. There is no cease-fire. There's no holiday season. For our American soldiers, the holiday season is lonely and hardly celebrated. Units do as good a job as they can and ship in delicious food and decorate the dining facilities and offices with holiday decoration. But for the soldier, it's a sad reminder that they aren't at home with their loved ones.

And for the wife at home, who has to muster all of her strength to ensure that holidays like Christmas are still a happy and memorable occasion, the overwhelming feeling of guilt and sadness linger. It's hard to feel joy and motivation to celebrate the holidays when your soldier isn't home.

The house is decorated. There are presents under the tree. The traditions are still being practiced, but the military spouse is sad. And she can't be sad in front of her kids. She can't be sad in front of the young wives during the unit holiday party. She tries not to be sad.

Being emotional was understandable, but unnecessary.

The seasoned military wife has learned to compartmentalize her feelings in public, especially during the holiday season. There's nothing more heartbreaking than seeing a military wife cry in the Target sales aisle during the holiday season.

What a seasoned military wife has learned after being at war for 10-years is this: she doesn't need anyone to feel sorry for her or her family. What she does need is the strength to be strong for her soldier, family, and the young military families who see her as a role model. She needs support from her family. And she needs faith to believe that he will come home safely.

Like her soldier, the military wife is conditioned to drives on! She turns the mental switch of sadness into mission essential survival mode.

She decides that while the situation isn't ideal for her family, she commits to living in that moment for herself, her children, and the military wives around her. While her soldier is missing all of the memories being made for his children, she commits to ensuring that his presence is still felt and that the children learn grace and gratitude for his service during the holidays.

She musters the strength of the military wife-warriors of generations past. She commits to spreading joy. She commits to finding an ounce of happiness. She commits to making every holiday the best. She commits to making every holiday the best. She commits to making every day the best! She commits to making every day count since it's another day closer to her soldier being home.

The holidays worldwide are a time of joy—to the military wife, it's her commitment to spread that message because she knows firsthand the sacrifice her soldier is making for that joy

"When my soldier got home, he told me that he had to mentally prepare for a family dinner."
—Military Wife

"I was happy that he was home, but now "I" was going to have to change everything. I had to prepare to allow him to reintegrate into the family."
—Military Wife

Chapter 12

The Homecoming and the Adjustment

Redeployment and reintegration; these two words could easily be interchangeable with war and peace. One of the greatest challenges for a soldier and his family after redeployment is reintegration. After ten years of being at war, the reintegration phase became more complicated.

With time, there is change. Separation forces change to occur for survival. With that change, systems are put in place to adjust. And that is what the military wife did to survive.

How do you change those systems when the family dynamic changes? The systemic pendulum swings up and down when the soldier comes home from deployment. Can the family change back to a cohesive unit when a soldier comes home?

For some, reintegration and adjustment are understood and expected. When soldiers and families stay connected and communicate prior to the soldier's redeployment, the change back to a cohesive unit happens seamlessly. Unfortunately, when expectations aren't discussed and communication is sparse during a deployment, reintegration isn't as easy.

For some, reintegration and change come with friction. It's like putting a square box into a circle. With enough friction, the square will chisel into a circle and forcefully fit, but it isn't a smooth transition to get the square in that circle. What some military families will find is conflict: the military soldier struggling to fit into the new family system, and the military wife having difficulty loosening the reins to allow the soldier back into the family dynamic. In the military lifestyle, change is inevitable and guaranteed. Success of the family is defined by how the soldier and family react to that change.

How does the military wife deal with reintegrating her soldier into a life that she's created without him? How does she surrender control to allow her soldier to come back into the family unit that has modified their way of functioning? How does she allow the soldier to now be a primary decision-maker in the family when she has made sole decisions without compromise?

The media does a fantastic job of portraying the "welcome home" ceremonies as tear-jerking and heartfelt. Tears and hugs and the American flags were all indicators that our soldiers—depicted as heroes—were home.

Early redeployment ceremonies showed soldiers disembarking from planes onto the flight line, and families running onto the runway to find and hug their soldiers. We were happy that they were home.

Fast forward ten years, redeployments were slightly different. Soldiers were brought to a big hangar or gymnasium to be released to families. The banners and signs were still present. The band still played. The soldiers were home but instead of being excited about the welcome home ceremony, they were impatient. They were anxious to be released and go home. Families were happy that their soldier was home, but nervous about the reintegration. So, there was a mixed bag of emotions at welcome home ceremonies 10-years after the war.

A Venn diagram consists of three circles that equally intersect. The three circles in the military life are the soldier's circle, the wife and family circle, and the military circle. In the military lifestyle, the circles occasionally intersect. If they do, they are connected with serrated lines. The serrated lines are symbolic of the many times that the military life disconnects the soldier from his family. No matter how many times the soldier tries to connect with his family or with the military, there is always some factor, be it a training exercise or a deployment or the stress of death in the unit, that keeps the soldier from connecting completely.

For months, while the soldier is deployed, the wife has lived a completely separate and /individual life. She developed relationships with neighbors and made her friends. She created her routine. She orchestrated a life that functioned without her soldier. She developed systems to operate with one less parent/partner. And she was successful.

And like his wife, the soldier built relationships with other soldiers in his unit. He was working all of the time, and his day-to-day experiences were separate from hers. His life was very different from hers. Months of separation lead to a lifetime of individual experiences.

And with redeployment, both soldier and wife had to figure out how to connect their two, separate life circles to create one whole life again. Will the circles intersect or will they simply live side-by-side never connecting? This same song and dance played on repeat during the GWOT years. The first week of a redeployment is identified as the honeymoon phase. Everyone is happy that the soldier is home. The soldier, wife, and children are hopeful that the transition will be successful.

The second week of redeployment poses to be more challenging. This is where the wife starts to recognize the signs that the soldier is different. He likes moments of quiet. The chaos of the day-to-day schedule and all of the moving pieces within a normal active household overwhelm the soldier.

The soldier is impatient. Simple requests to pick up the kids, to carpool, to rake the leaves, to wash the cars seem overwhelming. The wife suspects that the requests of going to the grocery store is a welcomed task because the soldier is alone without any chaos.

Loud noises and pops would immediately startle him. He's physically present, but mentally still far away.

Driving—well—being in a car with a recently redeployed soldier is like being with an Indy 500 race car driver. The seasoned military spouse learned to head caution when allowing the soldier to drive immediately upon redeployment. The rules of driving engagement for a soldier while they are deployed is very different from the normal Department of Transportation rules and regulations.

As for social integration, it's very hard for the soldier to interact with strangers that became his wife's friends during deployment. These are friends that she connected with that the soldier may have nothing in common with.

The soldier becomes socially selective, often opting out of social events, especially events with large crowds.

And sometimes, for the soldier, talking to civilians unassociated with the military was difficult. There were often questions about the deployment or his opinion about the government and primary leaders. While the soldier tried to reacclimate to being home, the last thing he wanted to do was relive his recent past.

With time, he adjusts, but the initial months after redeployment are challenging.

As for the military wife, she is cautious of what she said or did, knowing that the soldier had a hairline trigger that led to impatience and frustration. She accommodated the soldier's need for a slow and quiet adjustment back into the family. She is patient with the soldier's adjustment hoping this would synchronize the family rhythm.

And so, with the redeployment, there's compromise. Instead of planning an elaborate family vacation to Atlantis in the Bahamas or Disneyland, the family would plan a trip to the beach. Instead of having a humongous "welcome home" party (unless by request of the soldier), the family would have a small barbecue with approved guests. Instead of going bowling or to the Fourth-of-July celebration, the family would go on hikes and watch Independence Day celebrations on television.

One would argue that reintegration was easy and that their soldier blended back into the family as if he wasn't gone. Others would argue that their soldier's reintegration was a slow process and that it was a collective effort of every member in the family to encourage adjustments.

And then there are some military families that just didn't fare well. This unfortunate truth happened often around the midpoint of the Global War on Terrorism.

When two lives have grown comfortable operating separately and neither soldier or wife is willing to compromise and work together at change, then the efforts to reintegrate fail. During the midpoint of the GWOT war, this became very evident with our military families.

Surviving reintegration and adjustment to life away from deployment was another battle for the soldiers. This was the war a wife fought for her family.

2014–2018

For the GWOT children

"You were asked to grow-up too quickly."

"You are the toughest kids in the world."

"The question was never IF our soldiers are going to deploy. At this point, the question was WHEN are they going to deploy again?"

"You had no choice but to follow orders and go."

-Military wife about her children

Chapter 13

Another Deployment? Game Time

Osama bin Laden was killed on May 2, 2011. We were ten years into the war. Our soldiers were veterans of multiple deployments. They were seasoned and experienced. They were angry and tired. At this stage of their careers, they knew only how to deploy and fight.

The wars in Iraq and Afghanistan are hard on military marriages. At this point, the military wives that were still invested in the military lifestyle were emotionally sterile to deployments. And since the unpredictability of the military made it very difficult for the military wife to maintain a career, she became a professional military wife…this entailed knowing everything about the deployment sequence and how to prepare her children for another deployment.

There was the hope that deployments were going to be less frequent. Osama bin Laden was killed and soldiers were pulling out of Iraq, but there were no indicators that the deployment sequence was going to change.

Military wives were now seasoned veterans with three to four deployments under their belts. Like their soldiers, they became mentors for younger soldiers and wives. Their mission was now to prepare other military families for deployment. Seasoned military wives attacked a deployment pragmatically

And then there are the children. Military children are the military's pride and joy. From birth, military children are conditioned to understand one truth: that their father could die. And it is this very truth that forces the military child to mature quickly.

With every military move from one state to another, and with every deployment, a slight piece of their childhood disappears.

Military children are taught the importance of honoring tradition. They learned, through their father's example, about selfless service. They were raised to be patriots. They stood tall, put their hands on their heart, and honored the flag when the national anthem was played. They did this not because it's tradition but because they believed in the lives of generations of soldiers and patriots who fought for our country's independence.

The GWOT children became very familiar with deployment. They were able to comprehend what deployment meant and they had experienced firsthand the depth of sadness that comes with loss. The GWOT children had friends whose fathers or mothers were killed or wounded while deployed. They have been to memorial services and funerals.

Military children have seen more life and death by the time they were young teens than most normal teens would in their lifetime.

Unlike any other children, they were expected to take all responsibilities in the home required of them. They were trained to be mission essential pieces in keeping unit functioning.

From 2014 to 2018, it was common for the GWOT military child to have already experienced three to four deployments. While the soldier was gone, they knew they had to fill the responsibility gaps to help their mother survive. They weren't asked to take on this role; unfortunately, it became expected. And with every once of responsibility, they became bereft.

If encouraged to wake-up at 2 a.m. to snow plow the driveway after a snow blizzard, they did so with little arguing. When asked to make dinner for their siblings because mama needed a little break, they did it; no questions asked. They hugged everyone a little bit longer and argued with their siblings as little as possible so as not to upset the family harmony.

They asked for little and gave a lot. They learned to control their emotions. Never showing sadness or weakness.

GWOT children were asked to attend unit functions to represent their father's unit. They volunteered to hand out presents to little kids whose father was deployed for the first time.

They volunteered at the USO soup kitchen because they are taught that someone else may have been suffering more than them. This taught them gratitude.

They are patriots—confident, selfless, compassionate, resilient, tolerant, and mature.

They learned to appreciate the dollar because they know that the military life paid little even if their father worked a lot. So, they appreciate the little things but deserved so much more.

They became experts at understanding loss. They know firsthand that loss is part of life. For them, everytime they move, they lose their school and their friends. For the teenage, military child, they lose their teammates and coaches. For those that have girlfriends and boyfriends, they have to learn to say goodbye.

The GWOT military child had to grow up faster than most. They are mentally and emotionally prepared for deployments and all of the requirements that come with it. They made friends quickly and farewelled them just as quickly.

They learned the importance of appreciating life because of the uncertainty of soldier's survival while deployed.

And they learned how to accept death. They learned all of these life lessons before they turned eighteen.

GWOT military children were mission essential. They played a vital role during the deployment. They were taught to be contributing members at home so that a soldier can focus on the mission overseas and not worry about the family.

And because of the role the military child played during the GWOT era, they viewed their soldier's deployment as just another day at work, just another game. To them, a deployment meant game time. And they were critical players in the game.

For the brilliant women from Gray Wolf

All of your life you are told the thing you cannot do. All your life, they will say, you're not good enough or strong enough of talented enough. They'll say you're the wrong height or the wrong weight of the wrong type to play this or be this or achieve this. The will tell you no! A thousand times NO until all of the no's become meaningless. All of your life they will tell you NO, quite firmly and very quickly. They will tell you no . . . . and YOU WILL TELL THEM YES!
—Nike advertisement

From 2018 to 2020, I remember living next to some of the most brilliant women I have ever met. I was so impressed by their collective intellectual power. If we needed to start a small country, we could have easily sourced all of the professional positions. Ironically, only a handful of them could work."
—Military Wife

My neighbor's wives' professions:
Meteorologist, nurse, trauma nurse, psychologist, doctor, therapist, designer, artist, counselor, veteran, engineer, writer, teacher, fitness instructor, coach, master gardener, baker, dental hygienist, accountant.
-Military Wife, 2019

The Difference, written by COL S.A. about military spouses, 2001

Over the years, I've talked a lot about military spouses….how special they are, and the price they pay for freedom. The funny thing about it is most military spouses don't consider themselves different from other spouses. They do what they have to do, bound together not by blood or merely friendship, but with a sharp spirit whose origin is in the very essence of what love truly is. Is there a difference? I think there is. You have to decide for yourself.

Some spouses get married and look forward to building equity in a home and putting down family roots. Military spouses get married not knowing where they will live every two to three years. They will live in base housing or rent, and their roots must be short so they can be transplanted frequently.

Some spouses decorate a home with flair and personality that will last a lifetime. Military spouses decorate a home with flair tempered with the knowledge that no two base houses have the same size windows or same size rooms. Curtains have to be flexible and multiple sets are a plus. Furniture must fit like puzzle pieces.

Some spouses have living rooms that are immaculate and seldom used. Military spouses have immaculate living room/dining room combos. The coffee table has a scratch or two moving from Germany, but it still looks pretty good.

Other spouses say good-bye to their spouse for a business trip and know they won't see them for a week. They are lonely, but they can survive. Military spouses say good-bye to their deploying spouse and they know that they won't see them for months or years. They are lonely, but they DO survive.

Some spouses, when a washer hose blows off and their laundry machine doesn't work, call Maytag and then write a check out to get the hose reconnected.

Military spouses will cut the water off and fix it themselves because they nearest repair man is an hour away or because they don't have the money to pay for the repair services.

Other spouses get used to saying "hello" to friends they see all of the time. The military spouses are always having to say good-bye to friends made the last two years.

Some spouses worry about whether their child will be class president next year. Military spouses worry about whether their child will be accepted in yet another new school next year and if the school will be the worst in the city......again.

Some spouses can count on their spouses participation in special events..... birthdays, anniversaries, football games, graduation, and even the birth of a child. Military spouses can only count on the uncertainty of their soldier's participation because they realize that the FLAG has to come first if freedom is to survive. The military spouse accepts that it HAS TO BE THAT WAY.

Some spouses put up yellow ribbons when the troops are imperiled across the globe and take them down when the troops come home. Military spouses wear yellow ribbons around their hearts and they never go away.

Other spouses worry about being late for mom's Thanksgiving dinner. Military spouses worry about getting back from Japan in time for dad's funeral.

Some spouses are touched by the television program showing an elderly lady putting a card down in front of a long, black wall (Vietnam War Memorial in Washington, D.C.) that has names on it. The sard simply says, Happy BIrthday, Sweetheart. You would have been sixty today." A military spouse is the lady with the card, still dedicated to her soldier even after his death.

I would never say military spouses are better or worse than non-military spouses. But I will say that there is a difference. And I will say that our country asks more of military spouses than is asked of any other spouses. And I will say, without hesitation, that military spouses pay just as high a price for freedom as do their active duty husbands or wives. Perhaps the price they pay is even HIGHER. Dying in service to our country IS NOT near has hard as loving someone who has died in service to our country and having to continue to live without them.

God bless our military spouses for all they freely give. And God bless America.

Chapter 14

The Gray Wolf

Wolves are peculiar animals. They are pack hunters. Like soldiers, they operate as a team. They cooperate so that they can bring down large preys. And together, the pack operates as a unit.

Military wives are a pack of wolves.

In 2018, Blue Star (military families) revealed that in addition to the stress of the operational tempo of the military, two-thirds of military families were stressed about financial hardships. Half of the military families reported that it was difficult to make ends meet because the non-military family member was unemployed or underemployed (meaning that the military wife couldn't find work in the field she was trained in).

Imagine living a life where your partner is gone 70% of the time because of his job. Your family relies primarily on this income. Sadly, this income is just enough for your family to survive.

There are no unplanned expenses. For example: Major vehicle repairs or a child's sports equipment is an additional expense that requires funding reallocation. Even a Starbucks purchase is considered a "treat" and it could affect your bimonthly budget.

Bottom line up front, our soldiers are overworked and underpaid, and military wives couldn't find jobs to help with supplemental income.

Sadly, the only time a military family felt they were financially stable is when the soldier was deployed. Why? A soldier's hazardous duty pay authorized an additional quarter monthly earning to their normal monthly paycheck. So, a soldier's hazardous duty pay meant that a family could live a little less financially strapped.

Most families saved this supplemental income for a family vacation upon the soldier's redeployment. Others used it to pay off debt. And others, lived comfortably without their soldiers.

But deployments and hazardous duty allowances were sporadic.

How does a military family survive when their total monthly allowance skates the national poverty average?

How does a military spouse find employment or manage a career if there is a requirement to move every two to three years? Moving frequently became exceptionally difficult for licensed professionals (teachers, medical professionals, lawyers, real estate agents, beauticians).

How does one stay current and licensed every time she moves if each state has very specific licensure requirements? And by the time a wife completes her licensure requirements, takes the exam, applies for licensure (all out-of-pocket expenses), and is hired, she will only be in the position for a couple of months before it's time for her to move again.

Here's some interesting facts:

- 92% of military spouses are women
- 31.6% are underemployed
- Military spouses make 26.8% LESS in their job than that of her nonmilitary peers
- 35% of working military spouses require licenses (which often don't transfer across state lines): doctors, nurses, lawyers, teachers, therapists

And herein lies the double-bind: the impact of a military wife's career on her family obligation. Being married to a soldier begs the wife to do some self-reflection: what is more important "right now?" Is her career and her personal and professional happiness more important than being solely responsible for managing her family's happiness since her soldier is gone all of the time? For a generation of women encouraged to find career success and independence, a military wife marries into a very traditional, patriarchal lifestyle that subscribes to the traditional gender stereotype roles. All too often, the soldier is the sole income earner. The wife, often, stays-at-home. This comes due to her inability to find employment and the home responsibilities that fall on her shoulders since her soldier is never home. If the wife is lucky enough to find employment, her income earned typically isn't equivalent to her skill-set level of training. And the income earned doesn't offset the cost of childcare. So, typically, the wife will elect not to work because the cost of time away from home versus the childcare costs plus the stress of managing a house independently is difficult to maintain.

A wife's self-identity is then intertwined with her soldier's. This becomes a great point of contention. Throughout her marriage, a military wife's career success and personal and professional goals becomes a secondary priority to a soldier's career goals and advancement. This is an ongoing battle.

It's a challenge for a military wife to maintain a career and manage a household when her soldier is gone 70% of the time. It's merely impossible for a wife to maintain a career while her soldier is deployed.

Pyramid scheme companies preyed on the military spouse's desire to make a little bit of "pocket change." There was the false pretense of having "your own business and career" that appealed to the military spouse, since a traditional career wasn't feasible. There was never any shortage of Avon, Mary Kay, Tupperware, Scentsy, LuLaRoe, Thirty-One, or Longaberger Baskets representatives having parties disguised as spouse get togethers. With hope and curiosity, military spouses supported one another and purchased items. But support was partially out of desire to help the spouse build her business and possible desire to becoming a consultant herself. In the end, the revenue earned versus the finances invested were never equivalent.

This inability for personal and professional growth, self-discovery, and goal satisfaction can lead to depression and resentment.

There's a small percentage of military wives that have been able to manage some semblance of a career while being married to a soldier during the GWOT years. But even then, the military wife has to sacrifice those goals to manage household responsibilities or must discover other means of childcare support if the soldier is in a position that requires him to work 18-hour days or is deployed. The military wife has to reassess her goals and redefine her definition of success.

From 2018 to 2020, Gray Wolf Street on Fort Drum, New York, had a collection of military wives whose resumes were so impressive that they could literally run a small country. This collection of military wives collided in this time and space creating a self-sustaining support network during deployment and a national pandemic.

They were strong, smart, and confident women, from different backgrounds and with very different skill-sets placed together in rural, Upstate New York. Their soldiers were in primary leadership positions, deployment was inevitable, and employment was scarce.

What is the cost of being married to a soldier? The payment ends up being the military wife's career and personal identity. She supplements this payment with adjusting her goals to fit the demands of the military lifestyle. If she subscribes to the military lifestyle, she redefines her understanding of success and finds unpaid employment as the primary care provider for the family.

How does a strong, smart, confident professional woman transform all of her knowledge and education into the responsibilities of being a successful, professional military wife? What is the definition of a professional military wife?

First, the military wife acknowledges that managing a career is almost impossible while being married to a soldier. That is an extremely difficult pill for a military spouse to swallow. She has to admit to herself that her personal and professional goals are very difficult to attain, especially since her husband's military career takes him away often. Thus, she absorbs all responsibilities associated with the home: bills, maintenance, carpool, parent-teacher conferences, sport events, school extra-curricular activities. If the military wife can accept that a majority of the household responsibilities are hers, then she finds that her time is committed to the operations and logistics for the family. Some spouses have been able to find employment and are able to balance the home and work responsibilities. But, there is a greater percentage that aren't afforded such luxury.

So, while the military wife is not the CEO of a major company, she is the executive leader of her home and mentor of the operating systems for the junior military spouses in her soldier's unit.

Secondly, the military wife learns to skillfully craft her professional training to fit the military lifestyle. For example, teachers can become substitutes without having to file for state licensure. Media specialists (marketing, public affairs) can volunteer to work with the unit and run the social media platform. Business and logistics specialists can run successful fundraising events for the unit. Photographers and artists create unique military gifts and become self-employed entrepreneurs. While the employment opportunities aren't ideal, the military spouse acknowledges that her skillset can be a great contribution to the military community. She has to be cognizant that the time she spends offering her skills will most likely be voluntary services. Is she OK working for free? Is she OK working for very little money? Is she OK just finding a job that has nothing to do with her training?

Thirdly, the military wife survives as a chameleon, morphing into someone new with every move. In order to acclimate to new environments, the military wife has to be comfortable with cultural change. Each duty station is different. Each unit is different. Each spouses' support network is different. Resources are different. How a unit and installation conducts business in Hawaii is not how it is done in New York or in Europe. And while the military culture's roots are dug in tradition and uniformity, there are still recognizable differences at every installation when a military family moves. So, it is the military wife's stressful duty to ensure that her family is ready to adapt. Change is definite in the military, and so the military wife has to accept and become comfortable with change. And it is the time committed to this change that eventually fills the time that she no longer has to focus on her personal and professional goals. And accepting this fate is the double-edge sword for the military wife.

Lastly, the military wife must accept that the educational debt she acquired while completing her degree or trade will be a looming debt inherited by her AND her soldier. This fact requires the military spouse to swallow her pride. She learns that she may not be able to pay off her educational/training debt independently or as quickly as she would like if she were to find a job and start her career. If she didn't marry a soldier and moved every two to three years, her career ambitions may be attainable. This very inability to take full responsibility for personal debt can be a point of contention for any relationship. This becomes even more true for the military wife. She has to accept that she is now indebted to the soldier. He is the primary means of income for the family. The military wife finds that her income is earned as the primary household manager.

The greatest struggles for the military wife is posed with these questions: What can the military wife do with her life after years of unemployment, underemployment or sporadic employment? Does she have the courage to explore new career goals in order to rediscover her self-identity?

It is on the onus of the military wife to accept her fate. She represents the military and the unit in the community by volunteering for special events. She advocates for family services when they lack funding or don't have services available at all. She's a mentor. She's a teacher. She's an advocate. She does all of this voluntarily. And she supports the other military wives who struggle with the same self-identity challenges. She's a wolf, a member of the pack. But she's also a leader in the pack.

Some military spouses, toward the end of their soldier's career, will finally be able to follow their dreams. For years of her sacrifice, she now challenges the norm and starts the adventure for her career development. And this.....can be the first time a role-reversal occurs in a military relationship. For the military spouse who chooses a career profession requiring hours of commitment and time away from the family, the soldier is now responsible for managing the household. What does the soldier think when his wife is accepted to a school in a different state for six months? How does the soldier feel being a single parent of five children? What does the soldier do if he has to get the kids ready for school, but also has to work to prepare for the field?

Whatever the case, the military wife will always be an asset to the military. She will always be an asset to any organization and company that is willing to hire her. She's emotionally and mentally tough, intellectually competitive, a multitasker that doesn't understand the meaning of defeat, an organizer—disciplined, punctual. The military wife is a hunter and a wolf, again a member of the pack....a team member.

She does all of this understanding that the nation's security rests on her soldier's mental and physical capabilities. So, she inherently manages all stressors at home to ensure that her soldier can focus on his career.

The military wife, a gray wolf of the pack, works collectively with her military sisters, suffering and celebrating and rediscovering hidden skills and talents along the way.

"No matter where we come from, there is one language we can all speak and understand from birth, the language of the heart, love."

- Imania Margria, Secrets of My Heart

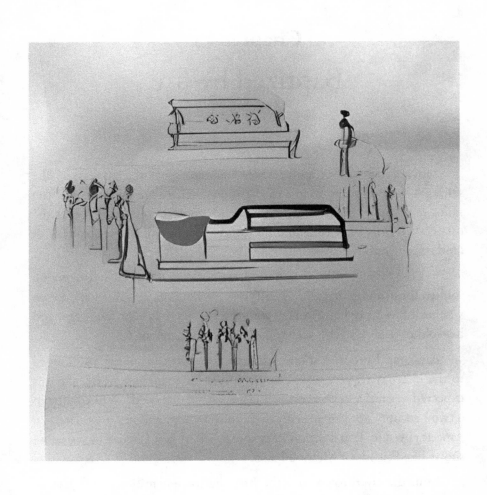

Chapter 15

Baptized by fire

Moving to another country where you don't speak the language is like sailing a boat into the middle of the ocean. There are no lifelines. The sailor relies only on the weather to steer the boat in one direction or the other. It is only with time and patience, that the sailor eventually finds land or sails into the abyss.

For the foreign military spouse that has fallen unlucky in love with a soldier, the military lifestyle is terrifying. What does a military spouse do when she has moved to a foreign country, doesn't speak the language, and her soldier deploys? This scenario occasionally happened.

A young, European spouse married an American soldier and moved to the U.S. With very little English in her language repertoire, she was expected to survive on her own while her soldier deployed. While living in a two bedroom apartment with no support, a dog, and her only friend in America lived in Texas, the military spouse self-taught English by watching shows like Friends or Melrose Place.

Immediately thrown into the fire, the foreign military wife had to learn true survival. She had to learn the language. She had to learn how to drive. She had to learn where to shop for groceries. She had to learn about the medical care system in case of an emergency. Oftentimes, she had to learn this all on her own.

This scenario is also true of the U.S. military spouse who have moved to a foreign country like Japan or Korea. She's asked to move to an apartment in the middle of the city. While the soldier is at work, the military wife has to discover how to maneuver through the city. She has to learn key phrases like, "do you speak English" or "can you help me" in a foreign language.

In both cases, the military spouse is often left to her own devices to figure out how to survive. While sponsorship is expected of the gaining unit, sometimes, the sponsor isn't married or has a spouse that isn't present to assist the family. So, again, the military wife is left to learn how to survive on her own.

Just like young military spouses are baptized by fire when marrying into the military, the flames are twice as hot for the foreign military spouse that has moved to the U.S. or the U.S. military spouse moving to a foreign country.

Now, imagine moving to a foreign country, not being able to speak the language and your soldier deploys. These spouses are twice as courageous and inspiring.

For Elaine: Battle Buddies for Life

I can't promise to fix all of your problems, but I can promise that you won't have to face them alone.

—Dandelion quotes

My battle buddy. My person. My friend.

I don't know how I'm supposed to sum up our eighteen months together on paper. Endless coffee dates, lunches, come-to-Jesus meetings at the battalion, by-invite-only gathering with our brigade sisters, phone calls to rant, date nights, birthdays, post and unit meetings with eye rolls and comments, baby showers, YOUR get-togethers (always a party, by the way), potlucks, selfies, selfies, and more selfies.

You taught me how to be a better leader, an encouraging mentor, and a more supportive military spouse. You helped me find my voice, supported my dream to reach out to the younger spouses, and helped them find their place. Your love knows no boundaries, your door is always open, and there is always a seat at the table.

Your love of life and love of all (well, most) things Army are contagious.

You make the days brighter, and deployments, field times, and late nights easier. Of all of the things I love about the North Country, you, my dearest of friends, made it unforgettable. ~Military spouse

Chapter 16

Battle Buddies

Some people are lucky enough to find their best friend when they are young. Best friends run through the gauntlet together: fights, boys, girls, driving, dances, drinking, getting into college, or getting arrested. That friend is your person. That friend knows all of the stories. That friend is the one that is either with you in Mexican jail or the one you call to bail you out of said Mexican jail.

Post 9/11, soldiers were ASSIGNED or paired with a battle buddy in their unit. The theory behind this assigned "battle buddy" was accountability. In practice, the battle buddies are supposed to take care of one another, protect one another, and make sure rules are being followed and that they are staying out of trouble. For all intense purposes, the Battle Buddy is a forced best friend. Through training, holidays, deployments, the soldier maintains his battle buddy until his next duty station, in which he will find another battle buddy.

And for the military spouse, finding friends, or even a battle buddy, every two to three years is a daunting task.

For the military wife, a battle buddy is a friend and confidant that can help her survive the stress of being in a new place, a new unit, training, and deployment. A military spouse battle buddy is a friend that the military spouse can call in case of an emergency and her soldier is not available to help her.

Imagine moving to a new place and not having any friends. Imagine moving to a new place and your soldier is in the field for 3-weeks.

Neighbors are unexpectedly anxious to greet your family with cookies and cards with contact information. Strange…why would you need the contact information for complete strangers? You have always operated independently and your family business has always been very private. Now imaging one of your children is very sick and you have to go to the hospital. Your soldier cannot be contacted, so you dress all children in their jackets, drive to the nearest emergency room in the middle of the evening. After waiting 2-hours in the emergency room, the doctor identifies that your sick child has to be admitted into the hospital. You attempt to call your husband on his cellular phone, and you discover that his cell phone doesn't get reception in the field.

So, you are in the emergency room with four children and a sick child that has to be admitted. Who do you call for help? This is where the military wife calls her Battle Buddy.

It's hard work trying to find the right fit, the right personality—the person who will keep you on the tracks so you don't go off the rails but will also stand by your side in a battle. The brutally honest person who will protect you no matter the price. The one that will cry with you when you need support. The one that will come over, no questions asked. The one that will just sit quietly with you. The one that will come to the hospital and help you with your children when your husband is unavailable to help.

For the military spouse, finding that person, her "battle buddy," is essential to survival. It is necessary to step outside of one's comfort zone and acknowledge that there is no shame or sign of weakness to ask for help.

The military life is so stressful. A battle buddy helps make the military life bearable. A wife's battle buddy doesn't have to be someone in the same unit. It doesn't even have to be a wife in the same brigade. It's the person you can call when you need guidance. It's that spouse you call when you're feeling sad or depressed or just need a person to hang out with. The battle buddy is the person you can lean on when you're being emotionally and mentally challenged. It's the reliable spouse that can be there to help in times of emergencies

So, it is very critical for the military spouse to find a friend. A friend who is willing to karaoke with her but also one who is willing to stand next to her at a memorial service and hold her hand.

Hold tight.

The military spouse battle buddy is not just the sister who is there through thick and thin for the two-to-three years on the installation, but that battle buddy can also be her military sister for life.

Hold my hand
Let's beat the odds together
Stay. Stay. Stay
Right here by my side
Don't ever be afraid
For I will be here
Always

—Unknown

Chapter 17

The Notification

There's no telling when it will happen. There's no way for a wife to be ready for that knock. Every day could be "that" day. The everyday stress of possible death lingers.

The military wife lives every day like it could be "that" day. Is it going to come?

Close your eyes.

Now imagine you just came home from dinner with your friends. You have just arrived at home and the children are already put to bed. You pour yourself a glass of wine because it's Tuesday and already the week has been a long one.

After watching an episode of Schitts Creek to lighten your heart, you finish your glass of wine and head upstairs to prepare for bed. You wash your face and brush your teeth. You put on your soldier's unit T-shirt, somehow feeling closer to him. And now it's time for bed.

You climb into bed, but you can't sleep. You try, but it's so quiet that you can hear your heart beating in your ear. You're leaning on your side, and you're staring at the empty pillow on his side of the bed. His face should be right there...but it's somewhere far away.

Your hand caresses his pillow. Tears rolling down your face. You're empty. You miss his snoring. You miss his sleep mumbling. You miss his smell.

It's late. The mind just wanders. It's 1:00 a.m. and you're still awake. You're finally sleepy around 2:17 a.m. You are struggling to stay awake, but then all of a sudden—

Knock! Knock! Knock!

Ding-dong!

You are immediately startled awake. You leap on your feet. What time is it? 5:30? 6:30? The clock looks blurry.

You grab your robe and run downstairs to find out who is at the door so early, and you try to prevent that person from knocking again so as not to wake the kids. Your feet are cold.

You look at the clock on the microwave. It's 5:38 a.m.

It takes a second for you to register the time. Why is someone knocking at 5:38 a.m.?

And you start to breathe faster.

Knock! Knock! Knock!

Oh, God! Why is someone knocking at 5:39 a.m.?

Your hands are shaking. You start to shake your head and then unlatch the dead bolt. Tears are starting to well up.

Your hand wraps around the door knob. You close your eyes and start to twist the knob. You hear yourself breathing. Your eyes are still closed and you hear the click. God please don't let this be......

As you pull the door open, you slowly open your eyes—

And there he was. You knew it was him. You couldn't register it, but you knew. When you heard the knock at 5:30, you knew.

The world around you collapses. YOU collapse . . . and he catches you. And for a second there's complete silence.

A deep breath and hot tears streaming down your face.

And then a shrill cry that shatters the spirit.

Your children hear your cry and come rushing down the stairs. Two gentlemen usher you inside the house. One guy embraces the children and attempts to soothe them; the other is holding you tight. You can't breathe.

It seems like hours. Everything is blurry, and you can't speak. You can't breathe.

Everything is out of control. The neighbor is now in the house. How did she know? She's taking the kids. Where are the kids going?

"Mrs. Gonzalez, can you hear me?" You're walking. Are you walking? You're now sitting.

"Mrs. Gonzalez, can you hear me?" You think that you nod. Tears are streaming down your face. You're still shaking. You don't understand. Someone is holding your hand while you are sitting. You blink and see the clock on the microwave: 5:46 a.m.

And, with every ounce of your strength, you open your eyes and stare into the eyes of the Casualty Notification Officer as the chaplain is holding your hand.

"Ms. Gonzalez . . . Nellie, the secretary of the Army has asked me to express his deep regret that your husband, Edward, was killed in action in Fallujah, Iraq, on November 10, 2004, during Operation Al Fajr."

Tears are welling in his eyes. You are trying hard to stay composed. The chaplain is still holding your hand. You can't breathe.

He swallows, and continues, "The secretary extends his deepest sympathy to you and your family in your tragic loss."

Tears are streaming down your face. You can't breathe.

There's a knock at the door. Who is that? What is happening? 6:07 a.m.

"Nellie, our Lord and Savior holds you. And will give you comfort."

The Chaplain is mumbling words. What are the words? What is he saying?

You can't comprehend what's happening, but there are three women in the house and another person. You know his face. He's in your husband's unit. It's Captain Scott.

6:13 a.m. You can't breathe.

One of the women starts hugging you.

"Nellie, Honey. We're here now. Don't you worry, Baby, we are here now."

It's Lesley. She's holding you close, and you cry louder. She's soft and soothing, and you know who she is. And she's here now. Your battle buddy is here.

Beth is in the kitchen. She finds the piece of paper on the fridge. And you see her. You can't hear her, but she starts making calls. Who is she calling? She has your Deployment Emergency Contact list.

And you see her calling. And she immediately follows the instructions on the list. The first person called, Eddie's mother. Beth is trying not to cry......Lesley is trying not to cry.

The Chaplain and the other uniformed soldier are up talking to CPT Scott. They are moving around the kitchen . . . are they making coffee? They are looking at the list, and they are making calls. I can't breathe. Lesley is stroking my hair.

"Honey, I'm here for you, sugar plum. I am so sorry, Baby, but we are here for you, and we will take care of everything. Beth is making calls, and going to get the coffee going. Erin is her, too."

She keeps holding me. She's rocking me. She's handing me tissues and forcing me to drink Gatorade.

Erin disappears upstairs. She gathers some clothes and a couple of toiletries and walks out of the house.

6:26 a.m.

Beth looks at you and gives you the slightest smile. She's still on the phone. Lesley is still holding you. She's asking you if you want anything? Coffee? More tissues? You just allow her to keep holding you, and you keep crying.

6:42 a.m. Erin shuffles the kids into the house. They are disheveled and frantically crying. And you collapse to the ground and open your arms, and all four of you hug and you allow yourself to cry. And nothing in the world makes sense.

Lesley and Erin are embracing you. And for that moment in time, all in the world is wrong and you just cry.

It's 6:46 a.m.

Chapter 18

The Care Team

On the day a spouse is notified of her soldier's fatality, two uniformed soldiers arrive to notify the spouse of the details of her soldier's death. Out of respect, the spouse is notified in person. The two uniformed soldiers are the Casualty Notification Officer and the Chaplain.

Within minutes of her notification, the unit contacts the Care team. This group of volunteer spouses provide complimentary assistance to the assigned casualty assistance officer. The Care team provides short-term practical assistance and emotional support to the family so that the family can function.

There are typically three volunteers per unit that rotate quarterly to assist families for about 3-days after a serious injury or fatality notification. These volunteers ensure the family has all that they need until immediate family support arrives. One volunteer handles contacting family members on the emergency contact list. That same volunteer also contacts the school and works to provide attendance guidance.

The second volunteer coordinates meals, cleaning, and transportation support.

The third volunteer is there for the spouse. She's there to help the spouse function and to be the source of comfort. She also assists the Casualty Assistance Officer with arranging the on-post memorial service.

These volunteers arrive immediately following notification and provide all of the logistical support to the household while the spouse is processing the soldier's fatality. What would a military wife do if it wasn't for the Care Team? How would she function?

The volunteer Care Team is a thankless job, but necessary to help the wife the first few days after being notified of the soldier's death. They are volunteers, and are a necessity for any and all units.

Only in the military community is there a system organized of volunteers ready to assist no matter how emotionally difficult the situation is to help another military sister they may not even know.

For T and P
For HV

For Goldstar families
Your sacrifice is never forgotten.

"Just like our eyes, our hearts have a way of adjusting to the dark."
—Adam Stanley

T & P's story

The scale of my life events have always tipped from one end or another on a pendulum. The way that I tried to maneuver through this military life was to bury my head in the sand and let life just keep rolling by.

The details have blurred with time, but it's an instance, like a song, a place, or an image, that immediately transports me to a time when P was here.

Any hopes that we had of our future with our boys was crushed the moment that I opened the door that Saturday morning at 5 a.m. It's taken me time, but I'm still learning how to make every day count . . . especially for our sons. It's P's bravery that has taught me that we are nothing more than the collection of experiences that makes us!

P and I are both from Monroe, NY. We were high school sweethearts. His father passed when he was six, so the only military influence he had was an uncle who had attended West Point.

While he was stationed at West Point, we decided that he was going to serve his obligatory time of five years and get out. So, I agreed that I would I apply for law school where he was living. I was currently attending law school in New York.

After West Point, he was stationed in Georgia, I applied to the University of Georgia. It was about three hours from where he was stationed, but we were close to one another. We were engaged shortly after I started law school in Georgia.

We got married in January of 2000. I graduated law school in June of 2000 and shortly after, P got orders to deploy to Kosovo. I didn't know anything about being a military wife. I moved to Fort Benning, and he tried to reassure me that everything was fine. That he was only going to be gone for six months. He also discouraged me from watching any movies like Black Hawk Down or Saving Private Ryan.

So, while P was gone, I did what I could to distract myself from him being gone and focus on the "here" to take the stress out of my mind.

When P was deployed, I met my first Army wife. She ended up being my best friend, my battle buddy. Neither of us had a military background, so we were maneuvering this life together. There was no internet, no cell phones, no computers. So, we got our information from the military community.

During the deployment, I dealt with it by focusing on my work and not thinking about the military. The entire time, I felt angst and dread, so I really put my energy in making a career work. I kept reassuring myself that if I had to maneuver my career to fit P's life, I could do it.

I was willing to sacrifice my sense of self and sense of goal.

This was my first introduction to how many women that had advanced and fantastic degrees were willing to sacrifice all of that for their soldiers and never use them.

With the military life, I never knew what was coming. I felt a feeling of dread that I did all of this . . . that I completed law school and did this for nothing, and that it's not fair.

And then September 11th happened. Our lives changed forever and fear took over me. We talked about our lives. See, P was initially going to fulfill his five-year West Point commitment and get out. It was September 1th that became the major life event that changed our life plans.

This is when I completely surrendered to P's military career goals. He was such a wonderful partner; he was worth it.

For so long, I believed I could operate by myself. It wasn't until I moved to Fort Drum that I really learned I was going to need fellow military spouses to survive this life.

In 2003 in Fort Drum, NY, our first son was born. I had to quit my job at our last duty station. I couldn't work because I didn't have a New York State license. But that was the least of my problems. We had just arrived in Watertown. We were living in a hotel, and P immediately told me that he was going to be deployed to Afghanistan. He was deploying three weeks after we arrived in New York.

The night before his deployment, he was very upset. Now we had a son. This made our farewell the next morning terrible. We dropped him off at the unit headquarters, and it was such a sad farewell. This was only going to be four-month deployment.

We were still living in the hotel when he deployed. It was such a lonely living arrangement. My in-laws had to come to Watertown to help me move to Sackets Harbor. So, there I was: new State, no friends, new baby, living in a hotel, and we had to move to a new house. Oh! And my husband was deployed to Afghanistan right after the 9-11 attacks.

The entire time, I lived in constant fear.

He returned safely, but it was only a matter of time before we started hearing about redeployment rumors. We heard that the next deployment was going to be a one-year deployment.

So, shortly after he returned to our new home, we had to say goodbye. This time, I had a tornado of events occur. I had a colicky baby, and my father got diagnosed with leukemia. I had to travel back and forth to New York City with a baby. On top of that, I was studying to take the NY State bar. So, in the middle of this one-year deployment, my baby wouldn't stop crying, my father passed away, and I was studying for and passed the New York State Bar. There was just so much going on that P's redeployment came quickly.. I was honestly so distracted that this one-year deployment came and went.

He was home for a year, and we had our second son. I started working, and thank God for the friends I made. I needed my friend to help me our children back and forth to daycare so that I could start working. I don't know how I could have done all of this without my military sisters.

Just as we had gotten comfortable and I had secured a good job, it was time to move.

We were stationed in Washington, D.C., for three years after New York. And after D.C., we lived in Kansas for a year. Although it didn't seem it at the time, living in Washington, D.C. was the happiest time of our lives. We were so busy (we both worked and P went to graduate school), but we were happy. After our short stint to Kansas, our family moved to Fort Stewart, Georgia in

2010. We were now 10-years into the war, and I had finally figured out the military. I felt a little better about this life. P immediately deployed to Iraq for five months shortly after we got moved in. He redeployed, and moved to an executive officer position in a unit that was deploying to Mazar-e-Sharif, Afghanistan. He was going to be in a staff/office position, so this made me feel better about his deployment.

Since the battalion commander spouse wasn't living in Georgia, I became the primary family readiness leader, which meant I was responsible for ensuring that all family members were being informed of updates from overseas. I was ready for this deployment. I was ready to be a responsible senior military wife.

We had great communication. There were computers and cell phones. I didn't have as much fear this time because P was a staff officer.

Any other time before this deployment, I had mentally prepared myself for the worst. His unit lost soldiers throughout those ten years, and I was somewhat prepared for anything to happen. This deployment, I didn't worry as much because he was just going to e a staff officer.

We spoke on his birthday, June 15. The details of our conversation are hazy now, but I remember it being happy. Our last conversation was on June 21. And then the doorbell rang . . .

June 22, 2012, at 5 a.m.

The doorbell rang. . . .

I wasn't prepared for it. Any hopes that we had for a future together was crushed the moment I opened the door.

As Americans, we are so lucky to be born with opportunity. P believed that to the bottom of his corps. He wrote this in an article about why he chose to serve in the Army during a time of war. He helped and made lives better.

His service was not without the ultimate sacrifice. But he believed in everything that he was doing and, as his wife, his dedication made me believe in him.

The details of our lifetime together have blurred a little with time, but there's always a song or an image that transports me to that moment when we were happy.

I've grown in so many ways since his death. I never could have imagined that all of my life experiences and training as a lawyer would bring me to advocating for military wives. Right now, I'm working on a portfolio to have congress reevaluate why the government taxes survivor benefits. Military wives have paid enough with the life of their soldier, why should their survivor benefits be taxed?

So, I'm an advocate for military spouses. I have found this to be my life's purpose.

This summer will be the tenth anniversary of P's death. I know he would be proud of me and the boys because we subscribe to making every day count. I value and love my time as a military spouse. It has made me the person that I am today.

I miss him . . . EVERY DAY.

—*T.V. Gold star wife*

H's story

He had the most beautiful and infectious smile. We met when we were both cadets at West Point.

When we entered into Active Duty service as young Army officers, the Global War on Terror was in full motion. As life would have it, we were separated often because of all of our individual training. And with two wars raging, we knew that we would be separated in deployment, too. But every situation made our reunions sweet. Every reunion felt like a honeymoon.

In 2006, I was deploying to Afghanistan. Later that same year, J was deploying to Iraq. Before he deployed, I was lucky enough to be home from deployment to kiss him good-bye. We knew that the dual-military soldier life was going to be tough. But it's never easy, regardless of what life you live, to say good-bye. J deployed to Iraq, and I was sent back to Afghanistan.

It was still early in the war, so communication wasn't great. Most of our communication was in email or letters. I was busy with my soldiers and he was busy with his.

November 15th, 2006.

I remember being asked to my battalion commander's office. I saw the tissues on the desk. He started slowly, and then he told me that J was killed. All I kept thinking was: I wish that I had my family or girlfriends here with me. I was in a foreign country, during a war.

I had no one to talk to; no one that I could unravel with because I was still in a leadership position as an Army officer myself.

I was sent home from Afghanistan for his funeral. We had a memorial service at Fort Bragg with his unit, and in December, we had his funeral at Arlington. Organizing the whole situation at Arlington was pretty messy at first because I was told that Arlington Cemetery was backed-up with funeral services and so J's wasn't going to happen for 6-months after his death. But, with luck and lots of support, we were able to have his funeral in December.

My leadership was very understanding. They asked me if I wanted to stay home and grieve and adjust instead of redeploy back to Afghanistan. I remember sitting at home, in an empty house, with no real purpose thinking: J is gone. All of our stuff is in storage still because we were both deployed. So, a couple of days after the funeral, I chose to redeploy back to Afghanistan to be with my soldiers.

It was hard for my family and friends to understand why I wanted to redeploy. They all encouraged me to stay home and grieve. But what I had found was: the BIG picture, with J's death, and me alone, was too overwhelming to think about. In Afghanistan, I still had a purpose, and that was to lead my soldiers.

I already had my spouse taken away. The Army was taken away from me when I left Afghanistan. My support network and friends were taken away because they were in Afghanistan. I realized that serving others and being really needed really helped me with processing both mine and J's greater purpose. I needed to take baby steps to get through each day; to get through each hour. And the Army and the people in the Army helped me with those baby steps. My Army family in Afghanistan, my friends, the soldiers, my co-workers, and my bosses help me with recovery. Baby steps.

And with anything in my life, the #1 thing shaping my worldview is my Faith. I asked myself, "Can I trust Him? Can I trust that God has a plan and something for me to do in this life after this tragedy?" I had grown stronger in my spiritual practice and fitness as a result of losing J because I did believe that God did have something for me to do here.

There's a string of unexpected blessings that have occurred in my life after J's death. I wasn't looking or expecting to find love again, but as God would have it, a kind act of concern blossomed into a friendship. That friendship and trust turned into a relationship. My heart started to fill again with the possibilities of love, and I'm blessed to say I have a husband and partner and a growing family.

Our dating situation, unlike other relationships, was pretty unconventional. We met while I was still an Active Duty Army officer, and now on my second deployment, but this time I was in Iraq. I saw him often at church, and we were lucky enough to attend several work meetings together. I was truly lucky to have a confidant and friend.

After traveling back and forth to see one another in our different duty stations, we were married in 2009.

There's this fantastic lie: You CAN have it all.

For the military wife, that's never true. When I got out of the Army, I attended graduate school, and I started to think about the military spouses and their lives. I was defined as a non-traditional military spouse: I was a soldier, a spouse, and I had a job. But a traditional military spouse has to try to manage a career and a family and volunteer at the unit. They shoulder so many responsibilities as unpaid volunteers.

So, with my experience, my points of contacts, and leveraging my understanding of the military, I started to think about how I could help military spouses. I started a nonporfit organization.

What's true about finding a job is this: it's all in who you know. For the military spouse who moves around a lot, the point of contact networks is pretty big and spread out throughout the world. This non-profit military spouse professional network helped spouses connect with one another as they moved from place to place. It's a trusting community that helped spouses connect with other professionals in different installations/posts all over the world. Because having to find a job or having to learn about a new state or country is much easier when you know someone. And so, that is what this professional network is: a group of professionals helping military spouses get acclimated or possibly find a job.

And so, what tragedy and this life has taught me is that life is about valuing the people and friendships along the way. You need your people to survive. You have to do this life together with your soldier and your friends. This life is a lot easier to maneuver when you know someone at the next duty station who can be there to help you....

In the military, you are never truly alone when something tragic happens. In this life, you will always have someone there to hold your hand.

-H.U. ~ Gold star wife

Taps

Day is done, gone the sun
From the hills, from the lake, from the skies
All is well, safely rest, God is night

Chapter 19

Spouses Sit to the Left

From 2001 to 2008, there were so many missions going on simultaneously. It was hard to track and follow them on the news. There were black-out communication periods that occurred often. Wives couldn't speak to their soldiers for weeks, sometimes months, when the soldiers were out on mission.

And when it was least expected, like shopping at Target or sitting in a movie theater or waking up at 5 a.m., either a call would come through disclosing the details of an incident or, worse yet, there was a knock at the door by the chaplain, the casualty assistance officer, and the notification officer.

Hold your breath. Close your eyes. And now exhale. Open your eyes.

Now, imagine the game of telephone.

One person starts a message and whispers it into someone's ear, who passes it along to another person's ear, who then continues down the chain. This practice is very similar to how the military was passing along information to the families when a serious incident occurs.

An incident would occur in the Middle East, and a serious incident report (SIR) was reported to the higher headquarters in the home station back in the U.S. The news would go from the higher headquarters to the unit rear-detachment, who would then pass the message along via telephone to the company point of contact, who would pass it along to the wives only AFTER all of the next-of-kin had been notified.

This whole process of finding out the details that are authorized to be released can take hours if the Army has a hard time finding or notifying the next-of-kin.

And that is how military spouses were told of a serious incident report and a memorial service.

Although military spouses may not know one another, unit memorial services are the one occasion most wives stop whatever is happening in their world to stand alongside and support their sister. From 2001 to 2008, the military wife attended more memorial services and funerals than most would ever attend in their lifetime.

The rigidity and formality of a military memorial service is what makes the service unique compared to a traditional memorial service. There's no talking. There's no moving. There's no lingering of soldiers or family members nervously joking or hysterically crying outside of the church.

As a wife walks up to the church, the first thing she notices is a sergeant and seven soldiers with rifles, standing at parade rest outside the church.

Walking in, two soldiers are handing out programs and directing visitors to the side of the church that guests are supposed to sit on.

On the left hand side of the presbytery, sits the unit chaplain, the rear-detachment commander, and a soldier or two designated to give the eulogy.

In the middle of the presbytery, there's a helmet resting on top of an upside down rifle, which is inserted in a fabricated rifle stand. Dog tags dangle from the butt of the rifle. A pair of boots are placed at the end of the rifle. The American flag is canted to the left and the unit flag is canted to the right. There's a picture frame of a soldier placed under the boots resting up against the rifle stand. It takes the wife a second to register the entire image as she moves to her seat.

Unit soldiers are directed to the far right side of the church. There, they sit upright, dressed in their Class A's. This uniform is equivalent to their Sunday best. It's proper to show their respects to the fallen.

Senior leaders, colonels, sergeants majors, and visiting unit senior leaders, and VIPS are directed to the VIP section in the middle of the church behind guests of honor. If the VIP is not accompanied by their spouse, they will sit on the far end of the pews.

To the far left of the church, typically starting five pews back from the front, are the spouses.

Military spouses sit to the left.

Since the right hand typically needs to be free to salute, it is protocol and etiquette to stand to the left. As in churches, buildings, and formal and informal situations, the military wife has become familiar with her position being to the left.

Connected by the bond of pain and tragedy, military wives stand by showing support regardless of their level intimacy with the widow. The military wife represents her husband and his unit, even when he's not present. She wears the unit pin on her left lapel proudly to show her loyalty and love.

She sits upright. She prays that she doesn't shed a tear because her heartache is nothing compared to the widow that lost her soldier.

They listen to the eulogies, bow their heads in prayer, praying for the widow's peace; praying for the children that have lost their father; praying for the mother who has lost her son; and secretly thanking God that they are not in the middle front pew. She hates herself for feeling this way.

"Please rise and bow your heads," the chaplain commands.

The chaplain gives the benediction and prays for the family, the wife, and the unit.

The entire congregation whispers, "Amen."

As the military wife has remained emotionally controlled throughout the entire service, her composure shatters as the soldiers come to attention. The first sergeant begins the roll call.

"Private Smith," the first sergeant calls out.

"Here, First Sergeant."

The military wife clasps her hands in front of her to stay balanced. Her knees are starting to shake.

"Sergeant Henry," the first sergeant calls out.

"Here, First Sergeant."

The military wife's eyes start welling. She swallows. She damns herself for being weak. She begs herself to stay composed.

She asks herself, "Why? Why am I losing control? I need to stay strong! Stay strong!"

"Corporal Thomas," the first sergeant calls out.

"Here, First Sergeant."

The military wife's lips start to quiver. She reaches for her sisters hand to the right, and they hold one another, trying to stand still, trying not to lose composure.

"Major Voelke," the first sergeant calls out.

Silence. The widows gasps. There's a faint whimper.

"Major Paul Voelke," the first sergeant calls out, again.

Silence. Now family members, soldiers, and leaders are all sniffling and breathing heavily.

"Major Paul C. Voelke," the first sergeant calls out with a little crackle in his voice.

"First Sergeant, Major Paul C. Voelke was killed in action on June 22nd, 2012," a soldier calls out.

"STRIKE Major Paul C. Voelke from our records," the first sergeant calls out.

Tears are now streaming down the face of almost every person in the church.

One, two, three seconds of silence—and then, "Reeeddddayyyyyy . . . fire!"

A loud shot echoes from outside the church as seven rifles fire simultaneously. The shot startles everyone in the church and all of the patrons flinch. One of the wives gasps in surprise.

"Reeeeddddayyyy . . . fire!"

The second shot of seven rifles fire simultaneously. Everyone stands still, anticipating the last round.

"Readddddyyyy . . . fire!"

The twenty-one-gun salute is complete and the lone bugler begins to play the haunting song of "Taps."

Muffled sobs. Gasps and whimpers. Sniffling and lots of tears.

Soldiers' hands saluting.

Military wives' heads bowed closing their eyes. Silent prayers and promises being made to God. Praying that God gives the widow peace. Promising God . . . just promising anything to God if He brought her soldier home.

As the Taps song slows to an end with the last note, she watches the widow and her family walk slowly up to the memorial display. The widow touches the dog tags, and she cries. Her children are with her, and they all hug, staring at their soldier's photo.

She begins her slow walk down the aisle out to the reception room.

The general and his sergeant major walk up together. They each grab a coin from their pockets and place it on the memorial box next to the boots. Simultaneously, they salute the memorial and then they begin to walk to the reception room.

All of the VIPs and remaining commanders follow suit. The soldiers of the unit follow the VIPs. And then there are the wives.

The wives wait until the end, as always, for the end of the service. They make their way down the aisle, and one-by-one, they slowly pause by the memorial to pay their respects. They say a silent prayer for the wife . . . their Gold Star sister. This branded awarded that no one ever wants but which few are unfortunately lucky to earn.

A wife asks God to give the widow strength to continue on. She asks God to give her peace with time. And then, with shame, she thanks God that the picture she is staring at is not her soldier's. She makes her way to the church fellowship hall to offer her condolences to the widowed spouse because that's all she can do.

She pivots to walk out, thanking God that she is not the widow.

While it's important to know where we come from and where we have been, it's more important for us to look at where we are going.

"How many times have you moved? My oldest son has moved four times in four years and attended four high schools."
—L.A., Fort Drum, NY 2019

Chapter 20

Suck It Up and Drive On!

In World War II, pilots that vomit in their oxygen masks had to "suck it up" or they would inhale the disgusting fumes. This expression became widely adopted as a metaphor by the military culture. The "it" in "suck it up" referred to almost anything.

For example: A soldier is tired on a road march and is unmotivated to keep walking. The sergeant will demand, "Suck it up, soldier, and drive on!"

This meant the soldier needed to suck up his pride and pain and keep walking.

How about a family infested with head live when the soldier is deployed? The spouse has to take sick leave from work for a whole week. All of the kids have to stay home from school. The military spouse has to burn sheets and towels. And all that she has to do is "suck it up, and drive on."

There's no better phrase more appropriate to define the temperament of the military spouse every time it is time to permanently change stations (PCS). Moving is hard. Even with the best preparation and organizational skills, it's still physically, emotionally, and mentally exhausting to move.

Now imagine packing up and moving every two to three years. The average military family moves ten times (yes, TEN TIMES) more than the average civilian family. And all that the military family can do is "suck it up and drive on!"

What would you do if someone told you that you had to move across the country in less than a month? Or better yet, what if you were given six weeks notice to move your entire family (oh, and you have a pet) to a foreign country? Oooof!

What do you call home?

If you were to walk into any military house, guaranteed that 60% to 70% of the homes will have some wooden placard with the hand-painted words "Home is where the Army/Air Force/Navy/Marines sends us" across the top. Attached with mini hangars are wooden planks that list the various duty stations that the family has been assigned to.

This decorative wall hanging is the family's badge of honor. In the military community, the more duty stations, the more credibility the family has. Basically, that wall plaque is an outward display to the world of how the spouse is able to organize a short notification move for her family and handle the logistical nightmare that comes with it.

When a military spouse is first married, moving to a military installation or somewhere in the town around it can be a fantastic disappointment. Unless your soldier is in the Marines or Navy (lots of duty stations by the beach), there's a pretty good chance that your duty station could be in the desert or the frozen tundra. This move can come with very real first-world problems where the nearest Target or Starbucks is forty-seven miles away.

Exploring new parts of the world can be exciting and a bucket-list adventure. Getting from point A to point B with an entire household of goods, finding new doctors, and registering kids and pets . . .that level of stress is unfathomable.

Let's start with the unknown.

All too often in the Army, a soldier doesn't know where and when he's supposed to leave. What is known is that the family has to leave and move to a new duty station.

What does the military spouse do?

Research the house.

Research the area and the schools.

Research driving/transportation options (some countries, you can't bring a car)

Research the hospitals and dentists.

Research the activities.

If you are moving to a foreign country: Do you have to learn a language? Do you have to have a specialty driver's license?

Research regional festivals/wines/restaurants.

As the American military wife moving to a foreign country, you have now become the family's American attaché. You are the investigative specialist responsible for researching all of the necessary requirements to get the family successfully moved to the foreign country. You are responsible for ensuring all of the passports are up-to-date, pet vaccinations are current, travel policies are read, and all school transcripts and records are available for the new school and hospitals.

And then there are the next-level elements of stress: your family has just moved to a new place. Your furniture and household goods are not being delivered for another month, and your soldier deploys within one-to-two weeks of arrival.

"We had just moved to our new neighborhood. We moved into or house in July 2011 and my soldier deployed in August 2011. We didn't even have half of our boxes unpacked before my soldier left. Our sons were six, four, and one."
—*Military wife*

By her third move, the military wife developed a system to move an entire house efficiently. She's learned which household valuables should be pre-packed prior to being packed. She's learned that about 7% of their belongings will be damaged or missing . . . so she accepts it. She is a trained Tetris master with her furniture understanding that every house she moves to is different. She can move from a 1800 sq. ft home to a 2500 sq. ft home to a 1200 sq. ft. home.

She knows who to call to coordinate move days. She knows when to disenroll the kids from school. She's made appointments for the kids' physicals so that they are done before moving. She knows when to disenroll the kids from the hospital and their dentists and requests records so that treatment at the next duty station can continue. On top of all of this, she's purchased gifts for all of the coaches and teachers of extracurricular clubs or volunteer organizations to soften the blow when she tells them that they will not be returning for the following season.

With every move, with every no notice change to the move, the military wife has to become the expert in Sucking It All Up and Driving On. And this is because she has to. Because there's no stopping—because she has to keep the military family machine moving. She is an expert at Sucking It Up and Driving On.

For Andrew, Jack, Brianna, and our military-child warriors

"Until you have a kid with special needs, you have no idea of the depth of your strength, tenacity, and resourcefulness."
—Anonymous

"As special needs parents we don't have the power to make life "fair," but we do have the power to make life joyful."
—Anonymous

August 2019

His smile lights up our world.

He's the sweetest boy, if he likes you. He will give you hugs and kisses. He's extremely smart.

Every day, I worry. I sometimes feel like a failure because I'm always getting pushed back EVERY FREAKIN' TIME we move.

Just when he is getting used to a routine and a teacher, it's time for us to move, and we have to start the process all over again.

First, I have to find all of his specialty doctors. I have to discuss his entire diagnosis and medical files with a brand-new care provider. And, while they are the medical experts, they are going off a chart and not what I know about my kid.

Second, I have to deal with the post. I have to figure out what after-school or post services are available. Each post is different, even if they are "supposed" to operate with the same basic policies and services. It is so frustrating . . . You'd think that I could seamlessly just transfer all of the notes from the previous post to the gaining post. Nope.

And then there's the school system. Damn. Every state, every post is different. They have different requirements, standards.

EVERY SINGLE FREAKIN' TIME! They always think that they know better than me, and I try to inform them what systems need to be in place for my child to thrive, but I get pushed back. I explain why these systems work for my child. And then I get pushed back.

"I have to do this EVERY single time we move. No one knows what my child needs more than ME. But every time we move, there's an assessment. Every time we move, there's a doctor that knows better. Every time we move, my heart breaks because this poor kid takes two steps back when he should be moving forward.

"And God forbid that my soldier deploys. I'm by myself, dealing with the bureaucracy of the state, post, community, and school. I'm advocating for my child and children like him by myself. And I fight every single time, by myself. And I'm tired. I'm so tired, and I'm sad . . . always so sad because all I want is the best for him. And right when we think we got it right, it's time to move.

Chapter 21

The fight for every day

Stability.

Stability is critical for a child's mental, social, emotional, and physical environment.

Consistency in medical support required for a special-needs child is exponentially more critical.

If you are a parent to a special-needs child, finding a medical specialist and support care is your number one priority. Your child deserves the best in health care, and attaining that can be the greatest triumph or heartache. The overall research, enrollment, disenrollment, reenrollment, and transition rests solely on the military wife because the time and the commitment it takes to find the right care is time that the soldier doesn't have.

A mother will go to great lengths to ensure the best quality of healthcare support for her special-needs child. With the military's bureaucratic insurance coverage, the military spouse has to request a referral for a specialty provider EVERY TIME they move duty stations. And EVERY TIME, prior to getting an appointment with a specialist, an appointment with a military primary care provider for an assessment is required.

This process is played on repeat:

Receive orders to a new duty station.

Request medical and school records to be forwarded to new duty station.

Request records and treatment to be forward to the next duty station.

Request exit consultation with all medical providers and specialists.

Move to a new duty station.

Schedule an appointment with a military health care provider for initial assessment to get referral.

Wait weeks for an appointment.

Move to a new home.

Request school assessment.

Go to an appointment for medical assessment.

Medical assessment results are similar to or differ from last assessment.

Request approval for referral.

Wait . . . wait . . . wait . . . for approval to be processed.

Three months after the move, referral request approved.

Schedule all specialty appointment.

Wait for results of specialty appointment to schedule follow-ups.

Assessment complete and future follow-ups authorized to be scheduled.

By the time the special-needs child receives proper services, there has been a two-to-three month disruption between services and treatment. And this process does not include requesting specialty educational services.

Special-needs and children requiring specialty medical attention deserve to have the best trained doctors and educators to assist with development. It's disappointing to disclose that there are no systems in place where medical professionals can immediately refer a special-needs child to a gaining doctor or therapist. As a matter of fact, sometimes, a diagnosis and years of therapy records are lost when relocating from one location to the next.

And then there are the inexplicable barriers. For some unknown reason, the barriers surface and affect moving forward with treatment. There are the teachers and therapists that "know better than the parent." They cooperate grudgingly, but not without advocacy from the parents.

By the time all assessments are complete, four-to-five months have passed after the move.

Championing the medical and therapeutic special-needs child's services is a full-time job. It can be daunting, but the military special-needs child will not receive necessary medical treatment without parental persistence. And this is twice as challenging when the soldier is deployed. There's no break for the military spouse.

The military special-needs mother is a warrior ready to protect the medical integrity needs for her child. No matter the amount of time, no matter the distance, no matter the cost, she will ensure that every ounce of her energy is dedicated to advocacy. And she does this again, and again, and again, in support of her soldier and the love for her family. And she does all of this mostly on her own.....

For M & D

"When it rains, it pours. And you don't have an umbrella. What do you do? Well, you turn the music up and you dance in the rain."
—Military Wife

From DL:

Today marks the ten-year anniversary of the end of "Don't Ask, Don't Tell (DADT)" in the US military. There are not enough thank-you's for all the people who worked hard to bring an end to DADT. Ten years ago, MK, while deployed to Afghanistan, quietly placed a picture of me on her desk. There was no hesitation on her part. I was the one who was afraid of how I might impact her career. I was the one who was afraid that coming out might make everything she'd worked so hard to achieve look differently from other people's judgmental lenses surrounding the gay community.

MK has always been and always will be a "go big or go home" kind of person. She has encouraged me these last ten years to embrace that same mantra. I'm not going to sugarcoat this business; I have sometimes really wanted to go home and hide under the covers, but going big has a way of becoming a habit. And yes, it has not always been easy. And yes, it did change the course of her career. And yes, it did change how some people treated us and interacted with us.

Even today, yes, it still feels like an uphill climb, but I wouldn't trade a moment of this ten years for anything. I'm proud to be a military spouse supporting my service member as they serve our country. I'm proud to meet people all over the world and get the chance to share a little of my rainbow-colored perspective on this crazy, trying, interesting, military life.

-Military Spouse

From MK:

Ten years ago today, I put a picture of DL on my desk while deployed to Afghanistan. This was how I came out to my unit. So thankful for having the best partner in life.

-MK, 2021, U.S. Army Soldier

"I choose you. And I'll choose you, over and over and over. Without pause, without a doubt, in a heartbeat. I'll keep choosing you."

Chapter 22

Don't Ask, Don't Tell (NO MORE), September 2011

In 1982, the military had a policy enacted that explicitly banned gay men and lesbians from serving in the military. In 1993, the Don't Ask/Don't Tell policy allowed homosexual and lesbian service members to serve as long as they were closeted. This policy didn't allow other service members to ask about a soldier's sexual orientation.

Suppressing their feelings mentally and physically affected these soldiers' mental health. Soldiers felt unsafe and feared harassment, and so, for many years, and still months, after the repeal of Don't Ask/Don't Tell, soldiers negligently expressed their feelings about their relationships.

In 2011, openly gay, lesbian, and bisexual men and women were permitted to serve in the military. Thousands of service members quietly rejoiced and finally allowed suppressed relationships to be introduced. Unfortunately, culture change takes time. There was still a lingering stigma and hesitation by many to integrate.

It took the military two additional years for military same-gender couples to receive spousal and family benefits. So it wasn't until 2013 that same-gender couples were authorized military healthcare and survivor benefits. Why did it take two years after the repeal of Don't Ask/Don't Tell for military same-gender spouses to get medical care? Why did it take two years for our country to authorize survivor benefits to a same-gender spouse if a fatality occurred? If less than 10% of the U.S. adult population serve in the military, should it matter what the soldier's sexual orientation is if they are willing to volunteer and put their lives on the line for liberty?

Maya Angelou wrote that "Love recognizes no barriers. It jumps hurdles, leaps fences, penetrates walls to arrive at its destination, full of hope." This couldn't be more true for all love, regardless of sexual orientation.

It's hope that the military keeps our country safe. It's hope that inspires our country's leaders to be wise and make decisions best for our soldiers. It's hope that keeps driving love—love of country and love of family, regardless of how we define family.

It's hope that our military will continue to grow in acceptance of our soldiers who volunteer to protect our country. It's hope that encourages our military culture to accept and not just tolerate soldiers regardless of sexual orientation. It's hope that inspires military wives to embrace the same-gender spouses who support their soldier and integrate those spouses into a world that is socially accepting.

Brave. There's no other word to best describe same-gender military couples who have stood on their principles to continue to love one another regardless of the scrutiny.

Patient. Same gender-couples have had to be patient with the military culture. Even more so, the same-gender military spouse has had to be patient with other military spouses to accept them. For years of being isolated and uninvited, the same-gender military spouse stood-by patiently waiting.

Patriot. While less than 10% of the country is willing to voluntarily serve the nation, the same-gender couple jumped into the flames of military service KNOWING that they may not be welcomed. Together, they believed that their duty to their country supersede the stress and challenge that came with unacceptance.

It's hope that our same-gender couples in the military will continue to stay courageous and grow as role models for generations to come. And that, in time, our same-gender couples and military culture will collide without fear of repercussions.

It has taken time, but our soldiers can now shamelessly serve the country they love with open support from their partner..

2021 marked the 10-year anniversary of the repeal of DADT, and today we celebrate!

For M and D…..thank you for being patient. Thank you for volunteering to serve our country. Your courage and patience is an inspiration.

For the Male Military Spouses

I can't tell you how many times our family goes out to an Army social or to dinner, and everyone always comes up to me and asks ME where I've been stationed. I smile and immediately say, "It's not me. She's the one in the Army."

The reaction that immediately follows is priceless: First, there's the apology. Then there's the embarrassment. Lastly, they are curious. All of this is always followed with, "So, what do you do?"

—Male Military Spouse

I am the most proud military husband. I stand proud knowing that my soldier believes in serving her country. And just because a patriarchal society looks at me and categorizes me as weak or soft, it doesn't mean that I'm not laughing at them inside and saying, I actually have the toughest job around.

—Military Spouse

Your grandkids are so cute. I cocked my head to the side and say, "Umm . . . that's my son. Yes, I'm older and, yes, my wife is a soldier.

—Male Military Spouse

Chapter 23

The Male Military Spouse

Parenting: the most important, thankless, rewarding job there is. In a lifestyle where the provider is traditionally a male, many would categorize the provider as the hunter and the wife as a gatherer.

The face of the military spouse is no longer just a well-dressed, poised, and polished young woman. The face of the military spouse now takes many shapes and forms, and noticeably different is the male military spouse.

While uncommonly seen, they are present. How to integrate male military spouses into a predominantly woman support network is a challenge.

While soldiers are in the field or deployed, military families sometimes migrate to one another and create life-sustaining support pods. Family play groups, outings, and dinners are common.

When the soldier is deployed, the male military spouse has to decide: Do I join the mommy-and-me group? Do I accept the invitation to the Spouses Club monthly luncheon social and bid on the spa day raffle basket? Will my presence be welcomed at the monthly unit spouses' Bunco Night Out or Coffee Group? Do I participate in unit activities and how will I be received? Will my presence be uncomfortable for the women if they want to complain about their husbands?

Toward the end of the war, the male military spouse population started to grow. There are always the looks; the suspicious glares from other people when they discover that the soldier is the woman and the man is the stay-at-home dad. This does not fit the patriarchal gender-role norm of the military. But, the traditional face of service was changing, and the military culture of acceptance started to change, too.

There are some military spouses that were overtly sympathetic to the male-military spouse. These are the wives that can't seem to understand, "how a mother could leave her children." Or they look at the male-military spouse and think, "if this life is hard for me, I can't imagine being a man having to deal with all of this."

A soldier is a soldier. Why is there such a different mindset about the parenting and survival capabilities of the male-spouse versus the female spouse?

For example: If a male soldier is killed at war, the phrase that crosses everyone's mind is, "his poor wife." But if a female military soldier were to be killed at war, and she's married to a male-stay-at home dad, everyone mutters, "those poor kids. How is he going to do it by himself?"

Why is there more sympathy for a military widower with children? Is it because society typically identifies stay-at-home fathers as less domestic and matriarchal?

The male military spouse struggles with being identified as the less-masculine stereotype. It's this stigma that deters him from participating in unit activities. And it's one of the many factors why the male military spouse shoulders all responsibilities without asking for help from other military spouses.

Regardless of what social event or support group the male spouse is invited to, acceptance is still a growing process in the military.

For the male military spouse, overcoming patriarchal gender norms, growing confidence in self-awareness, and being a champion in redefining roles to comfortably participate in a support group is a daily mental and emotional battle.

2018–2021

Chapter 24

The Perfect Storm

The Perfect Storm. That is what the year 2020 was considered to many military families. There were other colorful words and phrases used to describe 2020, but The Perfect Storm truly described the entire year for many military spouses.

For one group of military spouses, every hail pouring scenario was thrown at them. First, their soldiers were deployed. Second, they had to prepare for a snow blizzard. Third, in the middle of the snow storm, they were hit with a Pandemic: Covid had hit the country. Lastly, she had just been informed that her soldier wasn't coming home from deployment, but rather, he was being extended.

Military installations were locked down and families were required to stay isolated and quarantined. Schools were shut-down indefinitely. Families living on a military installation were ordered by installation leadership to isolate in their homes and not have communication with other families. It was March of 2020.

The military spouse was truly operating without her support network. She had the burden of homeschooling her children, communicating with other spouses via email or text, and the stress of managing a home while her soldier was deployed. And now, she was going to have to accept that face that her soldier wasn't coming home when she had planned. There was no end to the nightmare.

She had very little patience before the pandemic. Single-parenting had her barely hanging on. Covid chiseled away any remaining fibers of strength she had. Months of isolation without connecting and socializing with neighbors and friends affected her mental and emotional health. She operated on fumes 24-hours a day.

And she worried about all of it: her children, her soldier, the state of the world, surviving, and her friends and family. She worried about all of it and had control over none of it.

But in true military spouse form, she got creative. And she attacked each day with purpose to get to the next day.

She did all that she could to show her children that they were fighters and good citizens. She made trays of food for families who needed meals and dropped them off at door steps. She ran grocery errands for families diagnosed with Covid. She bought toilet paper and paper towels for friends. She made cards and delivered them to homes. She created fun days "in" instead of fun days out.

Covid was affecting everyone in the world. It had even affected our soldiers overseas. But at home, the military spouse was vigilant. She followed the rules as best she could to help her and her other military families survive. She fought the battle against Covid, home schooled her children, and acknowledged the extension of her soldier's deployment.

In the middle of the Perfect Storm, she survived because the military spouse is a fighter.

"Sometimes you just give everything you have, and you do your absolute best, and it doesn't stack up."-Tom Howard

I'm having a panic attack. I just realized that half of my life is over. I have a twenty-year-old son. I remember being twenty!"
—Military Spouse

Chapter 25

Fly Away

It's hard to believe that our soldiers were still deploying in 2018. What was the mission now? What was the operation called?

Soldiers who started in 2000 are now looking at five or six deployments under their belt if they were lucky enough to come home safely. They were home, but they were truly not the same soldiers who believed in and started at the beginning of the war.

This can also be said about the military wife. For twenty years, she has lived in a constant state of fear. But now, after twenty years of deployments, memorials, and transition, she's become an expert at compartmentalizing all emotion. So, now that fear isn't about the life or death of her soldier. The fear is: "So now what?."

On August 30, 2021, the United States Armed Forces started to pull out of Afghanistan, and she watched as twenty years of her soldier's sacrifice and dedication to democracy started to fly away. She watched on national television the hasty withdrawal and the wake of chaos to remove all U.S. Forces from Afghanistan.

And she watched her soldier.

How did twenty years pass so quickly? So much has happened. They have lived so many lives in many different places. The details of those lives are all blending.

She watched his face. She watched his shaking hand. She looked at her children, now young adults. Do they understand? Do they know the depth of the sacrifice? Do they know the depth of their father's commitment to the military, his country, his soldiers?

And she watched.

She watched the planes take flight with Afghanistan citizens begging to be rescued and given asylum. She watched as the Afghan citizens chased the plane down the runway screaming for help. She watched them hold on to the plane mid-flight.

And she watched.

She thought back to all of the soldiers. She thought about how much all of those young soldiers had seen and done in the early stages of the war. She thought about the caskets being brought home on the C17s. She thought about all of the young soldiers who tried to suppress and internalize all of that pain. Some surviving, mentally blocking those memories, but other soldiers held too tight to those nightmares eventually succumbing.

And she watched.

She thought about the wives and families and their sacrifice. She thought about the wives who started at the beginning of the war and decided that this military life was NOT the marriage she signed up for. She thought about the wives who supported their soldiers, sacrificing their careers and goals. She thought about the military wife's loss of personal identity, and how now, after 20-years, her identity as a military wife was flying away.

And she watched.

She watched twenty years of sacrifices and democratic efforts fly away. She watched military diplomacy fly away. She thought about the soldiers that paid the ultimate sacrifice. The families torn by the loss and hope fly away.

And she watched.

She watched 20-years of her life take flight. She wondered: now what? The stress of 20-years of moving, deployments, and crying with her military sisters is flying away.

And she watched

She looked at her children realizing that in a couple of years, they could be volunteering to serve in the military. She quivered at the thought of another war, now involving her children's generation. And her heart sank.

And she watched. And she cried.

And she hoped that this will not be something she has to watch again.

2021

"We gave everything we had. I can't be more proud of the effort we gave."-Hillary Witt

I don't know how my story will end, but nowhere in my text will it ever read . . . "I gave up."
—Unknown

Chapter 26

The toll of 20-years at war

In vino veritas. So be it....

One of my soldier's mentors said, "You know, son, I married an anchor. I felt weighted down. And that's why it didn't work. My marriage just felt heavy. You, on the other hand, you married a lifeboat. That's why it's worked this long. You're the lucky one."

There is no better compliment than this (well, ok! I'll also take, "you look amazing. Have you lost some weight?")

A lifeboat is a small rescue boat that is kept on a large ship and used in an emergency. They are sturdy and buoyant and used to save lives.

You couldn't have described the military wife any better than that...A military spouse is sturdy and strong for her soldier, her children, the unit spouses, and her military sisters. She's buoyant: staying afloat and riding wherever the wave takes her. She may not know the direction she's going, and she may not know what the weather is going to be like, but she stays-afloat ready to tackle whatever challenge lies ahead. She's lighthearted and cheerful because the life she lives is already so heavy and full of stress. She's a lifesaver: she is reliable, dependable, committed and selfless, ready to help anyone and everyone. She holds on to the ship of her soldier's career knowing that there are days where she has to save him from drowning in the stress of his day-to-day.

There is no greater love than that of a mother for her children...but there is no greater love story than that of a military wife and her soldier.

It must be love…love that motivated her to surrender to the military lifestyle. It must have been love that caused her to abandon her dreams to selflessly support her soldier. It is love that helped her stay courageous for 20-years in a military relationship.

I don't know what I thought being married to a soldier was going to be like. Fast forward 20-years, and here I am.

There are definitely days where I imagine what my life "would have been like" or what "I could have been" or even "what I could have done" if I had made a different decision. I would close my eyes and imagine the butterfly effect. How a minute change in my early stages of life could have dramatically changed the entire outcome.

But then I think about my marriage and our children and the amazing people I've met along the way, and I know this: I may not have become the woman that I thought I was supposed to be, but I have become so much more than I had ever thought I could be.

I have no regrets!

It can be very easy for a wife to be resentful toward the military. It can be easy for her to be angry about all of the missed birthdays, anniversaries, playoff games, proms, graduations, and milestones. She can be angry at the soldier for all of the training and the late nights that he wasn't home. She can be angry at all of the last-minute change of plans. She can be angry at having to move to Alaska or Japan or North Dakota or Louisiana when she thought they were moving to Hawaii.

In the last 20-years, there are so many things that the military wife can be angry about.

This life is not easy. It sure as HELL is not easy. But, is life ever easy?

The military spouses I have met are some of the brightest, strongest, patient, and most dedicated women.

Somewhere, between saying "I do" and "What the F*ck?" these women became committed, professional military spouses. It is the military spouses from the GWOT generation that has had to learn the painful lesson at a very young age that most will take a lifetime to learn, and that is: LIFE

IS TOO PRECIOUS and TOO SHORT. And so she learned to adapt, overcome, and enjoy every moment.

I have been so lucky to live a life full of unexpected adventures. This life has taught me to love harder, hold longer, hug often, adapt quicker; and appreciate everything. I sing the National Anthem proudly. And I think about all of our soldiers and their families every day. I've learned to not sweat the small stuff. I've learned how to be brave and to take chances. I've learned to trust. I've learned that my dreams don't have to end with military life, but that I just have to modify them. And I've learned that in the end, getting angry does nothing but give you gray hair, put lines on your forehead, and makes every day NOT FUN.

My idea of success has evolved so many times. When I was younger, I thought that in order to have a happy and successful life I had to have a career, a big house, and a fancy car. Today, I don't have a career, but I have held many different jobs that has taught me perspective. We don't have a big house, but we have lived in many different homes in different countries. I don't have a fancy car, but I have one that has taken our family thousands of miles to see the world. And our children are brave, considerate, respectful, thoughtful, and good people. They honor the flag and are loyal to their friends. They adapt quickly. What more could I ask for in life?

This has been a very hard life to live, but I've loved it. I try to wake every day grateful. I sing in my car as loud as I can to share my infectious joy. I tell everyone that I love them because it's so much easier to love and live than to be angry and hate.

I don't know what is going to happen the next 20-years. We have a completely different journey ahead of us. I have lived many, little, separate-lives while being married to my soldier. I'm excited because we are finally ready to start our ONE, big life together.

In Arlington and many other U.S. military cemeteries throughout the U.S., spouses are buried in the same graves as their soldier. And as the sun rises, shining all of its glory on the names on the headstones of our fallen soldiers, there is nothing more poetic than acknowledging that the sun sets on the name of the military spouse that is on the back of the soldier's headstone. They served their country together. They are buried together. In the end, behind every married soldier, is a spouse that supported him.

Military Spouse Car
Karaoke Playlist

....because life is a song that should be sung every day....

Elle King & Miranda Lambert: Drunk

Martin Solveig & Dragonette: Hello

Adele: Easy on Me

The Killers: Mr. Brightside

P!nk: Beautiful Trauma

Green Day: 21 Guns

Toby Keith: American Soldier

Lewis Capaldi: Before You Go

Taylor Swift: Shake it Off

Miley Cyrus: Wrecking Ball

Nelly: Hot in Here

Journey: Don't Stop Believin'

Drake: Hold On, We're Going Home

Katy Perry: Firework

Def Leppard: Pour Some Sugar on Me

Hanson: MmmBop

Beyonce': Crazy in Love

Daniel Power: Bad Day

Ke$ha: TikTok

Dexy's Midnight Runners: Come on Eileen

Fun.: We are Young

The Flys: Got you

Shawn Mendes: In My Blood

Megha Trainor: Mom

Justin Moore: Why we drink

Thomas Rhett: Beer Can't Fix it

Florida Georgia Line: Long Live

Keith Urban: Who wouldn't wanna be me

Acknowledgments

Writing this book has been a labor of love. It was the military wives that I have been lucky enough to meet in this life that inspired me to take the leap of faith and share their stories. Thank you for helping me find purpose and the courage to proceed. Thank you for devoting your life to the military, so your soldier can serve.

Thank you to Louie and Samantha for pushing me to finish.

For sharing their time, stories, and experiences regardless of how painful, I must thank Shannon, Traci, Denise, Amy, Karyn, Jenny, Susan, Alex, Mary, and Ms. Jan.

Thank you to the Wescott Hills Way Crew, Team Reynolds, and Team Kashawlic. You have always been our steady support. Thank you for always thinking of us no matter how many moves we made.

Thanks to the EOC crew of Fayetteville, Jenni, Sarah, and Kwuan, and the Friday Happy Hour traditions that kept me sane during deployments and while I was studying for my clinicals. Those were some of the hardest days of my life, and I am so grateful to all of you for being there for me and the boys. Your encouragement kept me going.

To Maike, Erin, G2, and Mariska: wherever, whatever, whenever! I love you all. Thank you for pushing me to do this and for being my sisters. You are the best friends I could have only met by chance.

To Matt and Gretchen, you are the best godparents and the most amazing people. Your weekly calls and check-ups while Steve was deployed really motivated the boys. They never laughed harder than when they spoke with you, and that made my heart full. We love you both.

To Lesley, for always finding a way to meet me anywhere to just hang. You're the absolute definition of a loyal and best friend. Our friendship was forged with our mutual hate of group projects. Fast forward to dogs peeing on Christmas trees, a pirate wedding at the edge of the earth, and getting kicked out of a hotel in Denmark because someone pulled a fire alarm....you are my sister. Thank you for always believing in me and for always pushing me to do what I love. You and Brandon are the most amazing couple, and I'm excited for your next adventure. A special thank you to Brandon for all of the art in this book. You are so gifted and the best, adopted Uncle.

To Cathy E., Doctor! Doctor! You are the coolest person. I wish I was as cool and level-headed as you. Thank you for inspiring me to be fantastic and for helping me realize that it's never too late to follow my dreams. You have helped me laugh during the toughest of times. I aspire to be more like you every day.

To Beth, for being one of my oldest and dearest friends. You're a marathon beast and an unbelievable mother. You're survivor and truly an inspiration. Thank you for being my best friend for over 27-years.

The Polar Bear Sisters, I am so lucky to have been a part of a group of courageous and devoted women during our last deployment. I couldn't have survived a snow blizzard and a deployment without all of you. You revive my faith in the Army military wife leadership. The Army is lucky to have a group of strong women to keep the flame going.

To the Gray Wolf, Wildwood, and Commando Sisters: Elaine, Steph, Stella, Meaghan, Andrea, Maren, Valerie, Karen, Katie, Heather, Bianca, Shelley, Mollie, and Kristen, Fort Drum was the best time I have ever had in my entire military spouse life. I couldn't have survived deployment and COVID without all of you. There will never be another collection of ladies in one place as good as we had it on Club Gray Wolf. Thank you for inspiring me, for supporting me, and for sharing that moment in time with me.

Honorable mention to Erich, who always made ten times the amount of meat he needed to feed our boys during their daddy's deployment. Thanks, Bro.

I know that I already mentioned your name, but Elaine, girl, thank you for keeping me on the rails. My train ride would have ended long ago if it hadn't been for your counsel and guidance. I love you and I'm so blessed that you are my battle buddy for life (whether you like it or not).

To the Dessert Divas 2.0, Erikka, Arpi, Sharon, Jenn, Jenny, Desiree, Michelle, Caitlin, Karyn, and Justina, thanks for making living in the middle of nowhere bearable. It would have been easy to just tuck my head away and not socialize, but you made the desert fun.

Thank you to Ms. Minnie Scott. You are who I want to be when I grow up. Your motivation and zeal to live the fullest life even after losing your love inspires me every day.

Thank you to my mentors who taught me how to be tough, graceful, gracious, and organized, and to embrace the title of military wife: Melissa, Shannon, Sarah, Erikka, and Julie. You will never know the impact you had on me.

Maurice, Tico, Kaylene, and Hadley, you will never know the depths of my love for you as our adopted family. Through the best and worst of times, you were always there for the Gomez family. Thank you for loving and supporting us.

And now my family—Mom, Ed, and Dex—I wouldn't be who I am if it hadn't been for you. You made me tough. You taught me how to be generous. You are always there when I need you. Thank you for always believing in me. I love you. Kathy and Adrianne, I couldn't have asked for better wives for my brothers and sisters-in-law. . It really takes a special person to understand the crazy of this family, but you are both amazing, strong women I am lucky to call family. Thank you for putting up with us. Dad . . . you always knew believed that I could be anything that I wanted. You made me tough. I miss you EVERY single day.

Peter, Barb, Gwen, Brian, Max, and Sasha, I am the luckiest woman in the world for having married into this family. You have always been there for me and the boys when Steve was deployed. Thank you for being our rocks and supporting us near and far.

And, of course, thank you to William, Quentin, and Matthew. You make my world so much more colorful. I am so lucky to be your mother, and proud of the men you are becoming. I hope all of your dreams come true. No one deserves a life of happiness more than you.

And to the love of my life, Steve, who makes it possible for me to follow whatever crazy dreams I have. From cake baking to fitness training to counseling to coaching to writing, you always supported me. Thank you for always being my biggest fan, and for inspiring me to do great things. I am the best version of myself every day because of you. I love you.

About the Author

Victoria Gomez is a Filipina–American military brat born in Fayetteville, North Carolina. She's the proud wife of a soldier and mother of three, bright, and amazing young men. Victoria has a multi-faceted resume: U.S. Army veteran, Pentagon policy writer, fitness instructor, substitute teacher, mental health therapist, Department of the Army equipment distribution analyst, NCAA recruiting compliance specialist, unit volunteer, team mom, coach, and university enrollment counselor. She's an avid journal keeper, lover of languages and cultures, car karaoke singer, selfie-taker, work-out-aholic, and traveler.

She enjoys writing whenever and wherever she can. She hugs longer, loves deeper, and laughs louder than most. She seeks every opportunity to make the ordinary extraordinary. She loves the beach, good food, football, and her family. She calls the world home.

9 781646 209156